"I had the pleasure of working with Dick for the first 2 years of my career. I was completely green with no field training whatsoever other than riding with other guys who were working. Dick was very knowledgeable and very patient with the new guys which made our shifts much more tolerable. During our tenure together, Dick not only provided public safety at a high level to the people of Cook County but also provided an atmosphere that was inclusive for everyone. I think back on those first couple of years and smile because I had a great role model to guide me."

Pat Eliasen, Cook County Sheriff

The events in this memoir are true glimpses into real-life deputy – community encounters. Events recalled by Deputy Dorr shed light on the relationships between law enforcement, their families, and the community they serve helping readers appreciate the challenges faced by rural law enforcement.

The North Shore of Lake Superior, known as a tranquil, forested area will surprise the reader. The wide variety of calls may even surprise veteran officers who may not realize the constant exposure to traumatic events experienced among the Northwoods. His personal relationships with friends and neighbors each day make being a deputy sheriff a difficult career. Few of us understand the emotional toll it takes.

Peter J. Mueller, Friend and neighbor

I have lived in Grand Marais for the better half of my life and so I have known Dick for thirty plus years. Knowing who he is and what he brought to this life of mine I am forever grateful. You may think living in this small town we call "home" would be without crime or heartache, but we have had our fill. Knowing that we were protected by this man gave us all a sense of peace. I have in my own family those who serve the law and the people in one way or another. I am looking forward to the book and would like to thank Dick for his friendship and service.

**Ann Jorgenson, Business Owner of
Java Moose and friend**

Many people say that they know and love the North Shore - the lakes and forests, the recreational opportunities, the artsy vibe - but they don't have a complete picture of the area. Dick Dorr understands the community, respects the wilderness, and has more than a few quirky, sad, and harrowing stories to tell about the people who live and visit Up North.

**Janet Simonen, Cook County Board Clerk/
Personnel Director (1988-2013)**

As a newcomer to Cook County, I appreciated the help and support I received from Deputy Sheriff Dick Dorr, both at work and at my home. Prompted by these law enforcement calls back in the 1990s, we got to know each other. As the years went by, I enjoyed his friendly visits to my office in support of ISD166 Athletic Programs. Thanks for you help, Dick! I look forward to reading your book.

**Sue Hakes, Former Grand Marais Mayor
and Cook County Commissioner**

We worked together for approximately 8 years so I can relate to some of the stories you have shared. This a great way to share your experiences of being a rural law enforcement officer. It provides the readers an opportunity to see what it is like being a rural law enforcement officer. I think the public, through the media and television shows, only see urban law enforcement. Your memoir provides an opportunity to show the differences and similarities, but also some of the unique calls rural law enforcement responds to. How you relate your experience growing up in a rural community and having a father who was a law enforcement officer and describing how that influenced you as a person provides insight into your career.

You were not afraid to share an experience that was embarrassing but taught a valuable lesson. It shows that we aren't perfect and that we can learn from our mistakes. Sharing the impact that being a law enforcement officer has on a family is important. It can be very difficult at times especially in a small town.

How wild the North Shore can be! Because we are a tourist destination it brings in all kinds of people. Because of your many years of serving the public to "protect and serve" you have many stories to share. Some can be mundane, very serious, unusual (killing the African lion), outright hysterical, and rewarding. The readers will love to hear the stories that you are sharing. This could bring a positive light on law enforcement, something that seems to be lacking these days.

I enjoyed the many experiences shared when we worked together. Law enforcement professionals are a close-knit group, even in retirement.

Mark Falk, Retired Cook County Sheriff (2005-2014)

"The value and impact of excellent law enforcement in Cook County, MN is illustrated through the personal experiences of longtime deputy sheriff Richard Dorr. The distinctive character of this place and people is brought to life through Dorr's valuable resource of historical records, research and stories."

Katie Clark, former Executive Director
Cook County Historical Society

My parents bought Golden Eagle Lodge in 1976. I moved here in 1980 and soon become a part owner. In 1982 I joined the Gunflint Trail Fire and Rescue squad which was a BLS (basic lifesaving) ambulance service as an Advanced First Aid responder. In 1984 I became one of 6 EMTs for our ambulance service. It's through this service, as a first responder, how I really got to know Deputy Dorr. We would see each other at all types of incidences, vehicle accidents, wilderness calls and drownings.

Deputy Dorr would make a visit to the lodges during his rounds from which I got to know him as an officer first. My dad wanted law enforcement to be seen at the business to deter illegal acts.

I became more aware of the care, kindness, and empathy that Deputy Dorr would have when I was with him on a drowning. I had recently finished some specialty scuba diving certifications, one of which was Search and Recovery. After a drowning that happened on Seagull Lake, Deputy Dorr asked me if I would dive for the body. Two canoeists had flipped, with one missing. The survivor of the two showed us on a map and pointed to where it all happened and told his story.

The party who picked up the survivor took us to the location. I suited up while Deputy Dorr gave me instructions on how he wanted the recovery done. Locate the body, mark it, come up, the boat would come over and then I would bring the body up face first to be able to take pictures before we removed it from the water into the boat. I located the victim in probably 15 minutes in 20' of water and followed the procedures that was asked of me. I gave a description of how the body looked and that he was laying prone on the lake bottom flat out.

After we had gotten the body in, Deputy Dorr went back to the surviving victim, and proceeded to ask more questions as the story didn't add up to what happened. The good swimmer drowns while the non-swimmer makes it to shore. No life jackets used. Canoe sinks with motor.

Deputy Dorr knew that because of the way the body was lying that there was likely substance involved. He was able to finally get the survivor to openly tell what substances had been ingested. Deputy Dorr was trying to make sure he had the answers with the investigation to understand why such a tragedy happened. He was kind and thoughtful to the surviving relative and knew what this person likely had gone through and didn't need the law to come down on him.

I saw from this incident Deputy Dorr's high standards in being human and a good lawman. He cared to get the answers so the surviving family could have closure.

Now after 42 years of being a first responder, I have worked with many types of law enforcement personalities. Deputy Dorr's humility, kindness, and understanding of a situation has always stayed with me. He demonstrated how to treat people during a crisis.

Dan Baumann, Owner Golden Eagle Lodge Inc
Gunflint Trail VFD President,
Fire Chief (12 years)
Assistant Fire Chief (past and present)
Senior EMT, CPR instructor

CHASING JUSTICE

RICHARD DORR

ISBN: 979-8-89079-275-4 (ebook)
ISBN: 979-8-89079-274-7 (paperback)

DEDICATION

This book is dedicated to Ray L. Dorr. My hero, my dad.
The man who was always there for me personally and with
great advice for me during my law enforcement career.

TABLE OF CONTENTS

COOK COUNTY SHERIFFS

1898	HANS GULBRANSON
1905	CLARK H. CARHART
1915	LEVER H. LIEN
1926	AUGUST J. JOHNSON
1926	LEVER H. LIEN
1928	LEVER H. LIEN
1928	AUGUST J. JOHNSON
1928	CHARLES E. TAYLOR
1939	F. C. "Cac" HUSSEY
1939	P. J. "Pat" BAYLE
1948	ALBERT J. MALNER
1959	ROBERT EMERSON MORRIS
1972	JOHN R. LYGHT
1994	DAVE WIRT
2004	MARK FALK
2014	LEIF LUNDE
2014	PAT ELIASEN

INVESTIGATIVE AGENCIES

DEA (Drug Enforcement Agency)
IRS
U.S. Postal Service
Minnesota State Patrol
BCA (Bureau of Criminal Apprehension)
FBI
Duluth Police Department
Brooklyn Park Police Department
St. Louis County Sheriff's Office
State DNR
State Park Service
U.S. Coast Guard
U.S. Border Patrol
Lake County Sheriff's Office
OPP (Ontario Provincial Police) (Canada)
U.S. Customs
U.S. Forestry
Michigan State Police
Superior Police Department
Minnesota Department of Revenue

FOREWORD

"Chasing Justice" by Richard Dorr, Former Deputy Sheriff, Cook County, Minnesota.

As I ended my 22 year career in law enforcement as a Minneapolis metro area police sergeant, I reflected over my collective experience of a total of 30 years in the army and as a police officer. The commonality of those in our shared profession is the altruistic motivation of service to something bigger than ourselves, helping those at a time of crisis and protecting the members of our communities in our respective capacities.

I spent the majority of available weekends and days off of my law enforcement career visiting with my parents who until recently lived in Grand Marais. Like most in the Minneapolis area, the North Shore was a convenient and affordable getaway for young families and my daughters and I took full advantage of the many camping, fishing and outdoor opportunities that Cook County provided.

Although I was a fulltime police officer and was always very mindful of my family's wellbeing and safety when traveling, I was always reminded of the law enforcement presence in the area including the Cook County Sheriff's Office, Minnesota State Patrol, US Border and Customs as well as the emergency services personnel who were ready to respond when needed.

Richard Dorr served these communities and visitors of Cook County from 1969-1997, having a vast timeline of real, tangible experience working and living within Cook County. Although a much different operational tempo than the Minneapolis/Saint Paul metropolitan area, Richard and his colleagues were not immune to the very real human nature that impacts our communities. Suicides, homicides, horrible traffic accidents and drowning all occurred during the many years of his service. That is the unfortunate reality of "the job" regardless of where one works. This lived experience can take its toll over the scope of one's career. However, it must be remembered that these traumatic events are balanced by the sense of duty and the accomplishment that comes with the successful resolution of conflict with people in crisis, saving the lives of others and making a distinct positive impact on the overall quality of life of the members of those communities we serve.

Join Richard as he recounts his vast experience serving these communities, both the positive and negative, and sometimes unreal. In a profession that has often been described as a front seat to the craziest show on earth, Richard weaves a timeline of his professional trajectory, sharing his personal experiences that will shed light on a profession that exists in all areas of our country to serve and protect.

Matthew T. Struck, MS, Retired.
Sergeant, Hopkins Minnesota Police Department

INTRODUCTION

Prior to moving to Grand Marais at age eleven, I had grown up with a father in the U.S. Border Patrol and an uncle who was the sheriff in Chippewa County, Wisconsin. Uniforms, badges and guns were a familiar sight for me. My first year in Grand Marais elementary school after our move there, my sixth-grade class had a tour of the courthouse offices. Part of the tour was conducted by the Cook County sheriff. Coming from a law enforcement family, I was familiar with men in uniform and can still remember how comfortable I felt that day. In addition, our sixth-grade basketball team was coached by a Border Patrol officer. My exposure to men in uniform continued to influence me.

Those influences eventually led me to taking a deputy position in Cook County in 1969 working for the same sheriff who gave my sixth-grade class the courthouse tour in 1959.

Cook County's unmatched beauty set the stage for so many interactions with law enforcement and first responders.

Why did I choose this career in law enforcement? Particularly in my hometown? Why am I choosing to write about my career after retiring? Many incidents took place over the years that I felt it important for both locals and newcomers to the area to know. Also, to explain what the police motto of "Protect and Serve" means to me. An obvious means of protection can be viewed by the weapons we carry. There are other ways we protect and serve. Has an officer served papers on you regarding a failing marriage or an inability to pay your bills? Has that officer spent an hour or two while you vented? Have you shared personal secrets with an officer? Has an officer consoled you after a death regardless of the cause? Has a loved one been saved from a house fire or comforted at an accident scene? Have you experienced something as simple as a warning when you ran that stop sign while late for work? As you can see and possibly relate to, there are many ways an officer protects and serves.

During my career, the men and women I worked with always did their best for the Cook County citizens. Some choices haven't been easy and we've all lost many hours of sleep due to worry. Ultimately, it's important to me that you know some of what has gone on in this area and continues to happen. The men and women behind the badge appreciate your understanding more than you know.

1

THE EARLY YEARS

I don't exactly recall the first time I saw my dad, Ray, in his police uniform. Ray Dorr was a young man who had returned home after fighting in the South Pacific during World War II. He was one of many men from the 32nd Red Arrow Division who were called up for the war from Chippewa Falls, Wisconsin. When the war ended and these men returned home, they set out looking for employment.

Chippewa Falls was a moderate-sized community on the Chippewa River in north central Wisconsin and home of the famous Leinenkugel Brewery. Post World War II days were busy days. Couples were reunited, there was work to be had and plenty of bars to celebrate new beginnings. Dad and his brother Cliff, who had gone through the war with him, decided to try the police department for jobs. In April of 1946, they were sworn in as police officers in Chippewa Falls.

This period in history is better known to us today as the Baby Boomer era. My dad did his share. He married my mother, Florence, a farm girl from Boyd, Wisconsin in January of 1945 and the following November my sister Janice was born. I entered the picture on November 10, 1947. During those early years, I remember my mother reading to me a lot, usually books about cowboys, firemen, or policemen. When I was four years old my dad would pop me up on his lap and tell me stories. I would touch his shiny silver police badge and listen to the squeak of his gun belt as he got up. It just couldn't get any better than that to this little boy. My dad was my hero and always would be.

After a few years on the job, Dad and Cliff started thinking there was more they could accomplish in law enforcement. Dad pursued a federal law enforcement career with the U.S. Border Patrol. In 1952, that agency was part of the Immigration-Naturalization Service. Border Patrol agents are armed mobile officers whose job is to apprehend illegal aliens who are in or attempting to enter the United States. In June of 1952, my dad left behind his wife and two youngsters to attend the Border Patrol academy on the southern border of the U.S. in Texas. There were no guarantees of employment as new Border Patrol candidates had to successfully complete the rigors of the Border Patrol academy. Aside from learning immigration law and the physical training involved, new agents had to learn Spanish. I recall my dad telling me how difficult it was in the Spanish lab busting his butt to learn the language while the Spanish-speaking candidates were throwing the football around outside. After getting through the schooling and two months of further training in El Paso, Texas, he was sent to his first station in Fabens, Texas. Once in Fabens, Dad sent for my mom, my sister, and me. We began our Texas adventure.

After my dad completed one year of probationary status in Fabens, his salary went from $3795 to $4205 a year! Back home in Chippewa Falls, my Uncle Cliff had pursued a different career in law enforcement. He had run for and was elected Chippewa County Sheriff. He was sheriff in the mid-1950s, and in 1958, he ran for a seat on the Wisconsin State Assembly. Cliff won that election, and his career became political, taking him to the state capital in Madison, Wisconsin.

Meanwhile, in the desert, our family had to adapt to a very different lifestyle. I was only a little over four so it was exciting to me. At six, I started school in Fabens and the kids all seemed friendly enough. I discovered how to break piñatas, dig tunnels in the sand, and fly kites using fishing poles to hold them. The desert was wide open and you could fly your kite almost out of sight. My mother, however, was getting tired of snakes and mice in our adobe-style house. I think my mother's recollection was that it was a "giant pain in the ass!" She would get frustrated going shopping too. The clerks spoke only in Spanish, and she was sure they were poking fun at her. Thinking about this from my mother's perspective, I think, "Hmm. First, I wait for this guy while he fights in a war for four years, then he comes home and drags the two kids and me down to this hell hole. It's gotta get better!" It did.

On June 17, 1956, my dad applied for and accepted a transfer to International Falls, Minnesota. We remained in Texas while my dad moved north to start his job and acclimate to a northern environment. He rented a room in a boarding house operated by a local football legend, Bronko Nagurski, a former college and professional football star. Dad wasn't there long before he found a house and sent for my mother, my sister, and me. Back we went to the north country and an entirely new lifestyle.

I went from flying kites in the desert to learning how to negotiate on a new surface. Ice! New to me that was. I was introduced to boots with steel blades and taught to chase a round black object called a puck all over a large sheet of ice-an ice rink I believe they called it. I should mention that International Falls is far north on the Minnesota-Canadian border, and people there take the game of hockey very seriously. It was a blast as I had some natural ability on skates.

I discovered Little League baseball and peewee football when the weather became warmer. My athletic ability made it easier to make new friends. Some of my childhood friends had great success with their sports. One of the boys I played hockey and baseball with was the great Tim Sheehey of Boston College and Boston Bruin hockey fame. Another thing I discovered in International Falls was the pecking order on being the new kid in town. I went to St. Thomas Catholic School which was across the street from the town's public school. The public school kids often confronted the Catholic kids at the end of the day. On some days, you had to fight your way home. That might have been my first introduction to bullies and appreciating fair play.

1958 Little League Team-International Falls

I can't speak for the government, but there seemed to be a plan in place for their employees. The practice seemed to be that an agent was to work in a community for three to four years and then get transferred to another spot on the globe. I suppose part of that thinking was to avoid agents living around locals too long and getting to know them well, perhaps to avoid compromising situations. Whatever the reasoning, it was hard on families. Of course, I was looking at it from the selfish eyes of a child, and I can't imagine how difficult our moves were for my mother.

June seemed to be the magic month. Perhaps it has to do with the fiscal year and how the government is set up to do things, but in June of 1959, we made what would be our last move as a family. I was eleven and my sister, Janice, was thirteen. It looked as though we would be breaking into new friendship circles once again. Our destination this time was

Grand Marais, Minnesota, a small town on the north shore of Lake Superior.

In 1959, Grand Marais was a town of approximately one thousand residents. It was a beautiful town right next to a natural harbor of Lake Superior. The town was laid out along Highway 61 which ran 110 miles west to Duluth and 38 miles east to the Canadian border. There were pockets of people located in communities all along Highway 61. Hovland and the Grand Portage Reservation were to the east, and Lutsen, Tofte, Schroeder, and Taconite Harbor were to the west. These areas were known as the East End and West End to local residents.

There were major inland roads in Cook County that started from Highway 61. The Gunflint Trail was a primary road going inland out of Grand Marais into the Sawtooth Mountain Range. This road was used in years past as a trail by Native Americans, trappers, and fur traders and ended at Saganaga Lake, fifty-five miles northwest of Grand Marais. It winds through the Superior National Forest and there were several lodges along its path in 1959. Other major roads to the west were the Caribou Trail out of Lutsen, the Sawbill Trail out of Tofte, and the Kramer Road out of Schroeder. These roads provided access through mostly state and federal forests to lodges, campgrounds, and logging sites. Another major road going inland also ran out of Hovland, a settlement eighteen miles east of Grand Marais on Highway 61. This road was known to locals as the Arrowhead Trail or the McFarland Road.

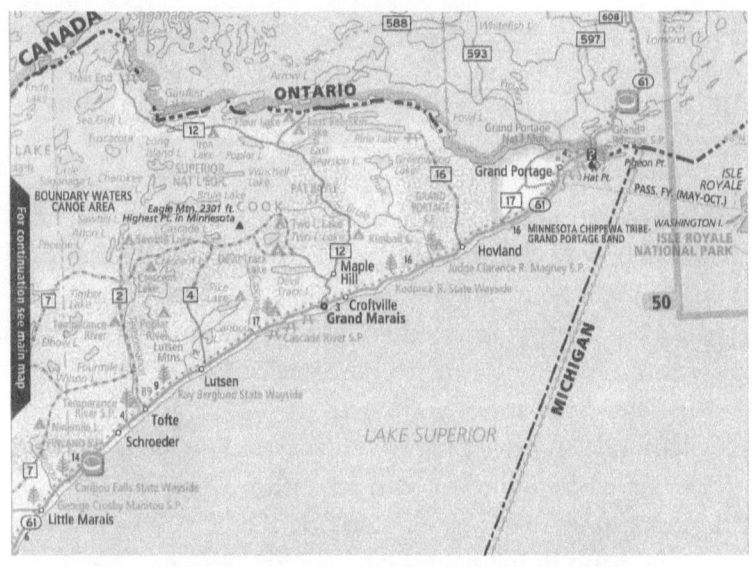

Logging and commercial fishing greatly influenced the area and added to its quaint reputation. A large privately owned logging mill operated approximately five miles north of town along the Gunflint Trail and employed many locals. Other than the fishing lodges in the area, tourists visited the ski hills at Lutsen which showcased some of the finest skiing in the Midwest. This was a major destination point for winter activity. Taconite Harbor was still a relatively new settlement thirty-one miles west of Grand Marais. A plant was built in Taconite Harbor to receive processed iron ore pellets and load them onto large ore boats that traveled the Great Lakes. There was also a power plant on-site to provide power to the Hoyt Lakes iron ore mine on the Iron Range. The processed pellets came from Hoyt Lakes and were transported to Taconite Harbor by train. This was a large operation that employed over a hundred people and created the need for living quarters, and a community sprang up. Then, an elementary school was built due to all the new children in the area. This occurred in the mid-50s and was going strong in 1959. There was enough work at this plant to provide jobs for several men from Grand Marais, and they made the sixty-two-mile round trip drive every day for over twenty years.

As a youngster entering sixth grade, my concerns were getting to know Grand Marais and meeting new friends. When you're eleven and haven't spent more than four years in any one place, it can take some time to adjust. Being new to the area, I wasn't aware that Grand Marais was a Nordic, close-knit community of people who had lived there their whole lives. Kids actually grew up with cousins and friends they have known since day one. I discovered the same pecking order existed here like the one in International Falls. Who the heck was this new, gawky-looking kid? That's what I was up against and didn't have a clue about.

Prior to moving from International Falls, my dad had located a house along Highway 61 just east of where the current Border Patrol station is located. In 1959, the Border Patrol station hadn't been built yet and the area around our house to the west or towards town was wooded. A dirt road ran east and west in front of our house parallel to Highway 61. This road, going west toward town, came out onto Highway 61 near the current NAPA store. I had been in town less than a week and was walking on this road toward town when I met my first obstacle-two boys, who I later discovered were a year older than me. They challenged my walking the road as if I had no right to walk their turf. I don't recall the exact discussion, but I do remember our meeting ended in a rock throwing fight. I was a mild-mannered kid but, God, I hated that bully mentality. Some days life was a bitch!

The road past my house had a driveway near the west end that went down a steep grade to a home near Lake Superior. One day, I met a boy near that driveway who lived there. He happened to be in my sixth grade class. He was a very nice, easy-going boy and a quick friendship developed. He introduced me to another sport that was very important in Cook County. Skiing! His name was Terry Cathcart, and he was an excellent skier. In the wintertime, he would create a slalom course on his steep driveway. I had been given skis by a border patrolman who worked with my dad and Terry taught me how to ski. I wasn't nearly as good a skier as he was, but I got to the point that I felt comfortable enough to go down his driveway and also ski the local ski hill located in Grand Marais on the area above the hospital. So, this road introduced me to a couple of knuckleheads and later, to a fellow student who would become a good friend. A lot like life-you get some bad, some good.

Grand Marais had a kindergarten through sixth grade school, a two-story brick building, where the current Harbor View apartment complex now stands. It wasn't much of a walk for me to go to school. It was a great old building with open staircases trimmed out in fancy wood top rails and large classrooms separated by cloakrooms. There were large, open windows allowing for plenty of light that made it enjoyable to come to this building. My athletic ability was an icebreaker for me with the kids in my class, especially the boys. Soon, I was the first one chosen when sides were drawn for games like baseball or softball. Of course, when you're eleven years old, you don't think about the kids who are chosen last.

International Falls had hockey; Grand Marais introduced me to basketball. In sixth grade, sides were picked and teams were formed. There were enough kids to make three or four teams. My dad bought our team red and white uniforms, and we called ourselves the "Border Patrols". We were even coached by one of my dad's Border Patrol agents. Instead of skating, I learned the finer arts of putting on an athletic supporter. I was twelve and one of the taller players so scoring came fairly easy. Our team won the sixth grade championship. It was a lot of fun that year and some solid friendships started growing. Sixth grade flew by, and my class made the transition to high school. The high school was three blocks north of Broadway Avenue. This school was for grades seven through twelve. The elementary school built in Tofte to accommodate the West End children went through grade six. That meant all these "new" West End seventh graders would be joining the Grand Marais kids in the high school. There were a lot of friendships made among the new classmates. Eventually, everyone was acquainted, and my recollection is of a nice group of classmates who became better friends with each passing year. We ended up with a graduating class of 77 students.

1959-60 6th Grade Champs-Grand Marais

Of course, during those first few years in Grand Marais, my folks were also establishing themselves in the community. They began socializing with the three other border patrol agents and their wives. My mom was meeting more people and seemed to be enjoying this new community. She got a job in the Cook County courthouse in the recorder's office. Several local women worked there, and my mom's social circle began to grow. My dad enjoyed hunting and fishing, and Cook County was a good area for that. Dad told me the story of when he inquired of the locals where there might be a good place to hunt or fish. They gave the pat answer, "up in the woods". In other words, "Figure it out yourself, pal!" Well, he did and soon thereafter, purchased a 12-foot Cadillac boat and a 7.5 Mercury outboard. We spent many hours together catching walleyes and shooting grouse in the woods. During the early 60s, there were several large logging operations going on in Cook County. New growth provided habitat for grouse, deer, and also the re-emergence of moose to the logging sites. That time spent together strengthened our bond and in those days of Willie Mays and Mickey Mantle, they couldn't hold a candle to my dad.

The most difficult and painful year for me was getting through ninth grade, that wonderful testosterone-filled period where every male is trying to get things figured out. I had a couple of classmates who were tough on me that year. The thing most kids don't realize at that age is that the mental pain they inflict with teasing lasts a lifetime. One of these boys came from a family with money and he was just spoiled. The other kid was the son of a businessman and had some of his own personal issues to deal with. They had grown up together and were longtime friends. Most of ninth grade I listened to them tease me about what they considered my physical imperfections. I could have kicked their ass on any given day, but it just wasn't my nature. I always found it interesting that someone who had his own physical issues would pick on someone else. Is that deflecting attention? It got to the point where I hated going to school because of the teasing. I remember asking my dad, "Am I funny looking?" He reassured me that I wasn't, but now, as a father myself, I realize how it must have hurt him to know I was being teased. All these years later, I can tell you those mental scars never leave you. As a ninth grader, you take the brunt of physical abuse from the upper classmen if you participate in high school football. I chose to take my angry feelings out on the field, and I really enjoyed the physical hitting. Well, that year passed.

The summer between my freshman and sophomore years, I got a job in the local care center as an orderly. I had compassion for the residents, and I learned several care procedures. In addition, I got to know several adults from the community who worked there. That summer, I grew from 5'9" to 6'3". When I entered school as a sophomore, the teasing stopped.

My sophomore through senior years flew by and I occupied my summers as a fry cook at the local A&W root beer stand. That business was located where the post office is today. Football honors and a state long-jump championship made me well-known in the community. My dad had turned down a promotion and another transfer in my sophomore year to allow us to stay in Grand Marais. We were starting to feel like we had roots somewhere. My mom left her courthouse job and went to work at the hospital for the administrator.

My sister, Janice, graduated in 1964 and married a local guy that same year. He was from the Hovland area and was very intelligent. He went to UMD (University of Minnesota, Duluth) and then on to the University of Oregon in Eugene, Oregon.

After I graduated in 1966, my mom took a position at the high school as the principal's secretary. Dad continued his work but discovered a new adversary-rheumatoid arthritis. He went to bed normal one night and woke up the next day to this life-changing medical challenge.

Because of my athletic success in high school, several colleges showed interest in recruiting me to play football or be part of their track and field program. I felt that I could play anywhere, but my grades and insecurities kept me from accepting any offers. Instead, I went to Ely Community College. My two years in Ely were once again marked with my athletic success. I had a casual attitude in the classroom, however, and didn't collect my AA (Associate of Arts) at this time. Things were heating up in Vietnam during the 1960s and being a mediocre student would get you drafted. It did. However, I didn't pass my physical due to an ankle injury suffered in football. I spent the summer of '68 in Grand Marais working for the U.S. Forest Service building campsites in the BWCA.

Forestry Days 1969

I entered school at UMD in Duluth in the fall. My dad recognized my casual attitude toward school and invited me

13

to start paying my own way. Given that discouraging news, I went to the St. Louis County courthouse, passed a civil service test, and secured an orderly position at a county operated nursing home in Duluth. My previous work as an orderly at the local nursing home in Grand Marais proved beneficial. I entered college as a night student and became a nocturnal human being. I went to classes from 6-9 pm and then worked the 11-7 shift at the nursing home. I'd come home, eat, go to bed, and get up at 4:30 pm, go up to the university library and study. Evening students weren't allowed to participate in athletics, so I maintained my nocturnal existence for that school year.

What's that saying? Too late smart. In retrospect, that was the best thing my dad ever did for me. I earned 34 credits and carried a 3.0 grade point average. After that year, I returned to Grand Marais to work the summer for the Minnesota Highway Department and think about the coming year. I had no specific idea as to what I wanted to do. Society was in turmoil with the Vietnam war protests getting worse by the week. Late in the fall of 1969, my dad came home from work and said "Emerson's looking for a deputy. Are you interested?" I went to the courthouse to speak with Emerson Morris, the sheriff.

2

STARTING OUT

S o, was it the memory of a four-year-old boy sitting on his dad's lap admiring the shiny silver badge or recalling the squeak of the gun leather as he tucked me in and went off to work? Could it have been my memory of the admiration that my friends had for my dad when he came home from work in his border patrol uniform, the gun, of course catching their eyes? I recalled it with a boyhood fondness and wanted some of that for myself. My reply to the sheriff was "When do I start?" December 1st, 1969.

Here I was, only three years out of high school, wearing a badge, carrying a gun and going forth into the community I had moved to as an eleven-year-old. I had just turned twenty-two but quickly became aware of the magnetism of the uniform. When I walked into a coffee shop, every eye was on me or so it seemed. Was it the uniform or the baby face wearing it? The awkwardness of public display eventually transitioned into a comfort level of sorts. As I began this new position, I met other law enforcement officers.

Prior to 1966, the village was patrolled by a constable. The constable was assisted from time to time by several local men. During this constable era, the patrolling officer was notified of a call by a rotating red beacon on the roof of the municipal building. The bartender took the call and turned on the beacon. The officer then checked with the bartender regarding the nature of the call.

In 1966, Grand Marais planned to establish a police department and had sent a local man for BCA (Bureau of Criminal Apprehension) certification. This man worked until November of 1966, then resigned. On January 1st, 1967, another local man was hired and sent for BCA training. During this period, Joe Jurek, a former Grand Marais businessman, was also hired. Joe's partner worked with him for several months but left for the Minnesota State Patrol, creating an opening for another patrol officer. Toward the end of 1967, the village did away with the position of constable and Joe became the Chief of Police. The old beacon method was done away with, and a police radio was installed in the municipal building. During the day shift, the city clerk was the dispatcher. Evening dispatchers were added. Stanley Suck was hired as a new patrolman on the police department. He had served military time in the community as a coast guardsman, met a local woman and they married. When Stan's military obligation ended, he moved to his hometown in Nebraska with his bride. He was working with the police department there when he saw an ad for a police position back in Grand Marais. Stanley applied for that position and relocated to Grand Marais. When he joined the police department in 1968, I used to visit him when I'd come home on weekends from college. As I got to know him better, I liked him.

In this era, when a new officer was hired, he was put on the street for a brief time period and then sent to a school sponsored by the BCA. These training sessions were set up in several parts of the state to accommodate the various law enforcement agencies. I was set up to go to the Alexandria

Minnesota Police and Fire Hall in March of 1970. That meant only three months on the job alone. What could happen in that time period? First, I became aware of how the sheriff's department operated. My boss, Emerson Morris, was a veteran of World War II and, as men of this era were inclined to be, he had many talents. He was a builder, a pilot, and a pretty good woodsman. He was not flashy and could be described as a private person. I don't recall much interaction between the police chief and the sheriff, but I do remember calls were dispatched from the sheriff's home by his wife, our dispatcher. The sheriff and his wife played things very close to the vest and guarded information when it pertained to the sheriff's business. The radio operated on the same frequency as the radio at the police department downtown in Grand Marais and information sometimes had to be shared by both departments. This was the beginning of a full-time police presence in Grand Marais.

Looking back on that time period, I think the sheriff had been operating as those before him, but times were changing and another deputy or two would have served him well. As it was, he seldom wore a sidearm in public but did have one available in his squad car. We also ended our shift at 4 pm when the courthouse closed for the day. That didn't sit well with the Grand Marais police who were trying to establish nighttime coverage. They felt the county was wide open after 4 pm.

The sheriff's office was in the basement of the courthouse, and I spent the first couple of weeks learning my duties, one of which was serving papers or legal documents that lawyers drew up and mailed to the sheriff's department to serve on individuals. This is called civil process serving. The sheriff or the deputy would serve the paper and fill out a return of service form with a service fee and mileage fee attached. The respective attorney or agency involved would then reimburse the sheriff's department. There are many types of papers and legal documents that are the sheriff's duty to serve. Another task I would have in the Spring of the year was conducting boat inspections of the many lodges in the area that rented out boats. That enabled me to meet the lodge owners and folks who lived in the back country. I also became more familiar with Cook County.

Tuesday morning, December 16th, 1969, began much like my first two weeks on the job. I arrived at the courthouse and continued to familiarize myself with the office and the courthouse staff. Then I got my first call to go to a residence just a few miles out of town and investigate a death. I think up until this day, the only deceased person I had ever seen was my grandmother in her coffin. The information I was given was that a woman was returning from shopping and discovered her husband dead in the house. The woman was with some of her children when they made the discovery and were gone from the home when I arrived. I cautiously approached the house not knowing what I would find and, quite frankly, not certain how I would react.

The setting was eerie. I slowly opened the door of the small house and entered. I observed the body of a person positioned upright in a wheelchair across the living room from me. As I approached, I noticed a long gun resting against the lower body of this individual. Getting closer still, I sensed I was walking on something crunchy and suddenly it dawned on me what had occurred. This person had shot himself and I was walking on bits of skull. Damn!! Nobody told me this came with the job. I composed myself and examined the scene more closely. The long gun was a high-powered rifle and had caused incredible destruction. During a background investigation, I learned this was a man who had been injured in a work-related accident over four years ago. He had been in severe pain for a long time and apparently chose to end it.

This case was determined to be a suicide and when the home was cleaned, the family continued to live there. As for me, I went home that night a different person. Even though there would be many more similar incidents to come in my career, none would be more graphic than this one after only sixteen days on the job. Looking back on that day, I've wondered why my boss sent me up to this residence alone. He was a long-time officer and certainly knew this family. I guess I'll never know. Maybe it was part of my indoctrination.

I continued exploring the county in my trusty 1965 International travel-all 4x4 truck. It had a four-speed on the floor and a police radio and that was it. It was green and was certainly better for backwoods use than running down speeders. As I was learning more about the physical county, I was also meeting its residents. It's amazing how narrow the scope of who you know is when you're just out of high school. Other than my classmates and some of their parents, the only adults I knew were some local business owners and some of my parents' friends. Throw a few schoolteachers into that mix and I had a lot of new people to get to know.

As I would soon learn, in a close-knit community, getting to know the people and how they're related can be a great help. I did take the opportunity to patrol the west end of the county and get to know the two part-time deputies. Fred Schmidt was an employee at the Taconite Harbor plant and lived in the thriving neighborhood community of Taconite Harbor. As the west end of the county developed, Fred became much like a constable of Taconite Harbor and was deputized in 1963. When I patrolled in the west end of the county, I always made it a point to stop and see Fred and his wife, Cathy. Fred was a World War II veteran and was easy to talk to and always ready to assist me. The Schmidts had several children who were in school the same time I was, and I got to know this family well.

The other part-time deputy was a member of an old Cook County family that was unique due to the fact they were the only African American family in the county. The deputy's name was John Lyght and he was deputized in 1968. His family settled in Cook County in the early 1900s. They homesteaded a large tract of land up the Caribou Trail out of Lutsen. John had several brothers, and they were large men in stature. After attending school in Lutsen, John went to work in the family logging business. I remember my dad telling me that one day while he was in his Border Patrol office, a woman came in looking somewhat upset. She asked him if he knew of any African American men in the area. He asked her why she wanted to know. She said her vehicle slid off the highway between the U.S. border and Hovland and that a logging truck stopped and several large black men got out, lifted her car back on the highway, then drove off without a word. My dad smiled and said, "You just met the Lyght brothers."

Seeing these large black men load a logging truck by hand became a local legend. John worked many jobs as a young man including caretaking properties, doing some fishing guide work, bouncing (keeping order) at the Lutsen ski chalet during dances, and driving school bus for the school district. My first contact with John was when he was our bus driver on several of our athletic trips when I was in high school. It wasn't unusual to see Fred and John patrolling the west end of the county together. It didn't take long for me to sense things weren't warm and fuzzy between these men and the sheriff. It seemed their independent patrol system threw a cog into the control factor the sheriff may have desired. At any rate, the first few months flew by as I continued my efforts to get to know the law enforcement personnel in the area as well as the citizens living throughout the county.

3

A LOT TO LEARN

Before I knew it, March 20th had arrived and I was enroute to BCA school in Alexandria, Minnesota. Alexandria is approximately three hundred miles from Grand Marais and by leaving two days prior to classes, I thought I would take the time to acclimate to the area. It is said "timing is everything" and only one day after my departure, a homicide took place in Cook County. During a domestic dispute at a home in Tofte, a community 27 miles west of Grand Marais, a woman stabbed her husband and he died as a result of the injuries. This would have been quite an experience for me and I missed it. Cases like this provide an officer an opportunity to learn investigation techniques, trial procedure, and to meet judges and attorneys.

Those of us attending BCA who came from a considerable distance were housed in the Viking Motel with an attached restaurant that had an impressive buffet. I was excited yet apprehensive about the days to come. Sessions began on March 23rd. Our instructors were veteran officers from large departments who were now employed by the BCA training division. There were twenty-nine officers at this particular session. In 1969, we were taught 175 total hours of criminal law, traffic law, self-defense, firearms, first aid and basic crime scene procedures. Before classes started, I met some of my fellow classmates and had an opportunity to listen to their experiences. Officers from Douglas County, Swift County and Glenwood Police Department knew each other as their departments were in close proximity. They would share war stories and talk about the different reports they were filling out and activities they were involved in, and I thought "Oh boy! This is going to be a learning experience."

I didn't even know what an ICR (Initial Complaint Report) was, so I just kept my mouth shut and listened. I quickly learned that ICRs were basic information reports filled out for each incident called in to your office for which you took action. The instructors were very good and I was a sponge taking in as much as I could. Of course, they had their own war stories that helped spice up the classes. I realized how much I had to learn. This was an era where women were starting to enter law enforcement but there were none in my class. After a day's session, it wasn't unusual to meet some of the instructors at the local Holiday Inn and get to know them better over a couple of beers or drinks.

Being in the Alexandria police and fire hall also presented me with the opportunity to meet some of the local officers. One particular police officer I hit it off with was an amicable man named Paul Anderson. I took the opportunity to ride a few shifts with him. His approach to the job was very professional and I learned a lot just observing him.

An evening I will never forget was at the Holiday Inn with the instructors. School had been in session for about three weeks, and we were all feeling comfortable with each other. As we sat in the lounge, a page came over the intercom requesting an officer or a doctor to the swimming pool area. Of course, we all jumped up and responded to the pool just in time to see a young boy being pulled out of the water. One of our most seasoned instructors started performing CPR on the youngster but couldn't revive him. The boy was between four and six years old and had slipped away from his family to the pool area. Shortly after this youngster was removed from the area by medical personnel, I saw our instructor break down. That reaction puzzled me at the time but as I continued in my career, that reaction was easier to understand when my own resilience began to break down. There was a somber atmosphere among us officers for the next couple of days.

Training progressed and I felt I was doing well. One of my concerns was how I was going to implement what I had learned when I returned home. My favorite session was coming up and that was the firearms class. I was a good shot as my dad had me shoot with him since I was twelve. I always considered myself trustworthy and safe when it came to firearms. The night before the on-range shooting was to take place, I was cleaning my weapon. I carried a model 15 S&W (Smith & Wesson) .38 caliber revolver. As I was finishing up, I was sitting on the bed in my motel room and a couple of classmates came in. "Dorr" they said, "We're going to kick your butt on the range tomorrow with our Colts." I responded "Yah, right!"

Like most motel rooms, this one had a long dresser on the wall near the foot of the bed. I had a full pop bottle sitting on this dresser. I had just cleaned my gun, so knowing it was empty, I raised my trusty old .38 and while aiming it at the pop bottle, I told my buddies who were standing at each end of the dresser, "I'm going to just squeeze the trigger and..." BLAM! My gun went off! It actually fired! My two classmates hit the deck, the pop bottle exploded and I threw the gun down on the bed in utter disbelief. This was impossible! I had just cleaned it and knew it was empty! I looked at the hole in the wall fearing I may have killed someone in the next room. A feeling of dread came over me thinking I had ruined my life.

I went out in the hall, took note of the rooms by number and went to the lobby. "Is anyone in rooms 'such and such'?" I asked. "Yes, they are all occupied" was the reply. Panic-stricken, I demanded "Give me the keys to those rooms!" Perhaps the clerk saw the terror in my eyes because she reluctantly handed the keys to me. I cautiously entered the room next to mine and called out, "Anyone in here?" No response. I peeked in the bathroom and there was no body. I heaved a sigh of relief. The bullet had blown the coffeemaker off the wall, and it was scattered all over the bed. No one killed or injured but the bullet went into the next room. I checked this second room and found it also empty, but the bullet entered and exited this room too. Continuing, I found all the rooms empty. This was probably because it was the dinner hour and apparently the occupants were out. The bullet was found in the wall of the corner suite so it never made it out of the building. I was thankful but felt certain I was going to be sent home or at the very least, disciplined in some way. This incident was investigated by the local police and was determined to be an accidental discharge. To this day, I don't know who interceded on my behalf. I wasn't disciplined and didn't even receive a bill for damages. The following day, an instructor said "I heard you had a little excitement in your room last night, Dorr." I did finish first in my class in the shooting competition. Since that day, there is no such thing in my life as an "empty" gun.

Another evening I will always remember was, once again, at this Holiday Inn. I was out with a police officer from the St. James Police Department. We spotted two young women sitting together at a table across the room. I told this officer,

"I'll flip you, heads for the blonde, tails for the brunette." I got heads and introduced myself to this young, blonde woman. That was on April 1st of all days.

Classes continued and I spent all my time studying and getting to know this little blonde I had just met. Her name was Laurie and she was a farm girl from central Minnesota. She and her sister, the brunette, had moved to Alexandria and were starting out in their own careers. Laurie was a nurse and was working at the local hospital. We spent hours in conversation and I was smitten big time!

As April ended, we completed our law enforcement training session. I did well and would soon go back to Cook County to work. Prior to my return to Grand Marais, I asked Laurie if she would marry me and she said YES! And so, the first four months of my career came to an end. I had worked my first suicide, seen my first drowning victim, shot up a motel and met my future wife. I still had a lot to learn but life was anything but dull.

BCA School 1969

4

NEW ROADS

Prior to leaving Alexandria and returning to Grand Marais in late April, I took the civil service test for a police position in Alexandria. My ultimate plan was to pursue a position with the U.S. Border Patrol. However, I wanted to create some options in case my plan failed.

Late April, May, and June kept me busy. The March murder case went to trial and a jury acquitted the woman who stabbed her husband in a domestic quarrel. She had originally been charged with 2nd degree murder. I served as a bailiff during the latter stages of the trial. May found me going into the backwoods to visit lodges and inspect fishing boats. I met the hard-working lodge owners and enjoyed discovering remote areas of the county I knew little about. Several of these lodge owners became good friends as the years went by. The Gunflint Trail, Grand Portage, Hovland, and West End residents contributed to their communities as emergency medical responders and firefighters. They also assisted deputies in the backwoods emergencies that we became involved in. Their knowledge of the forest where they lived was a tremendous aid.

Time went by quickly and before I knew it, June had arrived. Laurie and I continued our relationship long distance and had chosen June 20th to get married. We knew each other for less than three months but it just felt right. Even though it was the heart of the tourist season and I was the only full-time deputy, the sheriff granted me a week off for the wedding and honeymoon. The wedding took place at St. Thomas More Catholic Church in Lake Lillian, a small town just west of Cosmos, Minnesota, Laurie's hometown. She had a large family and we felt it would be easier for them not to have to drive the 300 miles to Grand Marais for the wedding. Unlike Grand Marais and the much cooler North Shore, this was central Minnesota farming country, and the temperature was in the 90s. Partway through our ceremony the elderly priest almost fainted on the altar due to the extreme heat of the day. My dad went up on the altar with a glass of water and helped revive him enough to complete the ceremony. After a reception at Laurie's parents' farm, we left for our honeymoon to the Black Hills of South Dakota.

Prior to our wedding I found a two-bedroom apartment in Grand Marais, one block from the courthouse and two blocks from the hospital. We were back in town setting up housekeeping and getting ready to go back to work by July 1st. Laurie went to work at the local nursing home which was attached to the hospital. She was earning about the same salary as I was so we felt good about our financial situation.

There weren't many young people to socialize with, but we enjoyed spending time with Stan, a Grand Marais police officer, and his wife. We also visited with Dan, the West End game warden, and his wife.

A difficult call came this summer on July 3rd. A six-year-old girl was struck by a car and was killed. The accident happened several miles east of Grand Marais on Highway 61. A Minnesota state trooper handled the call and I assisted with traffic. This little girl went to our church, and I recall a particular Sunday when Laurie was singing in our pew. This child just watched with such a wonderful look on her face as Laurie sang. That was a tough call to respond to. After that, every time I drove past that location, this little girl came to my mind. Some things stay with you longer than others.

The sheriff's department always responded to drownings. In 1969, we didn't have access to technical equipment for water recovery. The department had a set of grappling hooks which were large treble hooks attached to a metal rod approximately four feet long. The idea was to tow the grappling rod behind a boat and attempt to snag whatever one was searching for. We received a report of a man who fell out of a canoe on Rose Lake. The sheriff and I portaged in with a canoe and grappling hooks and attempted to locate this victim. We never did. It was quite difficult to work with grappling hooks out of a canoe. Heck, due to its location in the boundary waters, it was difficult getting to Rose Lake!

Another call we responded to was of a man who fell off an oar boat while docked at Taconite Harbor. This dock is a large cement pier big enough for an oar boat to pull alongside it. The surface of the dock is several feet above the water. When an oar boat is next to the dock, it is several feet up to the deck of the ship. If one was to go aboard from the dock, a ladder is put over the side of the ship and it's quite a climb up. The seaman who fell from the boat into the water took quite a fall. This time we used the grappling hooks while standing on the dock near the location where this man entered the water. We did make a recovery. This was the first time I saw a body being brought up from the watery depths. It is difficult to describe how uneasy that made me feel.

In October, the sheriff's department was notified of a drowning in Saganaga Lake at the end of the Gunflint Trail. Two brothers were reported missing after a windy day. A canoe and some of their gear was found washed up on shore. The area of the lake where they allegedly capsized was a large open body of water. We towed the grappling hooks behind a boat as if trolling with a giant lure. This went beyond the "needle in a haystack" theory but you do make an effort for the family. We never located these men. Death was becoming a common theme attached to this job.

Local politics entered my life in 1970 because it was an election year, a dynamic I had not even thought about. One of the part-time police officers was running for sheriff against my boss and I sensed most of the other area officers were supporting him. I campaigned pretty hard for my boss as I thought this part-time officer was kind of a blowhard. I had questions about his ethics based on an incident he took part in that went to his benefit over the public's. I mentioned my concerns to some friends shortly before the sheriff's election. I don't know if my criticisms swayed the election, but my boss won the election by a small margin.

It was November. My boss had been re-elected so my job was secure for another four years. My new marriage, the job, and the election all seemed to make the time go by fast. I was starting to wonder how long I wanted to stay in this work environment especially when I recalled my Alexandria classmates' stories of the police work they were involved in. I would ride with the Grand Marais police from time to time and as they patrolled during their shifts and interacted with the state troopers and other officers in the area, I felt this was more the type of environment I was hoping for. All the grumbling about the sheriff's department not working nights was getting old.

The straw that broke the camel's back came on New Year's Eve as 1970 came to an end. I had the day off. The next morning, I went downtown to gas up my vehicle and a station attendant asked me about a shooting in Grand Portage the night before. I came up with some kind of answer but the truth was, I hadn't even been informed of a shooting. As the only deputy in the county, I felt the sheriff should have called me to go with him on what turned into a homicide investigation. Nope! The sheriff had gone up to Grand Portage alone. I then discovered how the county handled this kind of call. A private investigator from Duluth was hired. When this man came to the county, the sheriff did send me with him to Grand Portage. I sat through the interviews, learned where several of the residents lived, and examined the crime scene. I learned from this case and established a friendship with this investigator. There was a murder trial and the 31-year-old shooter was convicted and sent to prison. While I was acting as bailiff during the trial, I had time to think about the way this investigation started and the fact that I hadn't been noti-fied when the shooting took place. Did I want to continue my career here?

I had a few credits left to obtain my associate degree from Vermilion Community College and felt it would be a benefit to complete my degree. I worked through July 1971 for Cook County and then resigned to go back to school. In September of 1971, Laurie and I headed off to Ely, Minnesota and I completed the required credits for my AA degree. Laurie did private duty nursing for a college professor's wife who had multiple sclerosis. After winter quarter, we moved back to Grand Marais intending to figure out our next endeavor. We lived with my parents three miles east of Grand Marais along Highway 61 near Devil Track River. Eventually, we heard about a young couple looking for someone to manage their cabins on the lower Croftville Road, a short distance from my folks' home. We rented the couple's home and took over running the cabins. Laurie went back to work at the local nursing home. I got a job dispatching for the Grand Marais Police Department. Dispatching gave me an opportunity to get to know the area officers better. I continued to learn through their responses to calls as they came in. The nature of a call was recorded in a logbook along with the time of the incident.

In the early summer of 1972, I took the federal service entrance exam in Duluth for a U.S. Border Patrol position. I passed and later was recalled for the physical and interview portion of the exam. I also passed that and was informed I was on a list of highly recommended candidates to be called to the next academy. So, I waited to be called. In the meantime, I received a call from the Alexandria Police Department. They had an opening and based on my civil service test, they were offering me a position with their department. It was a wonderful opportunity, but I turned it down waiting for the call to the Border Patrol.

In 1972, The Grand Marais municipal building contained the city clerk's office and the police station and jail. The city clerk acted as the daytime dispatcher. In the rear portion of the building was a room for officers and dispatchers. The evening and overnight dispatchers were also the jailers. The other half of this building contained the municipal liquor store and lounge. The lounge was very large and a popular place for locals to hang out. The standing joke was if there was a problem in the lounge, all the cops had to do was walk next door.

By today's standards, the setup for the jail wasn't very secure. An event occurred during the summer of 1972 that never happened before. A jail break! A runaway male teen was stopped trying to get into Canada. He was turned over to U.S. Customs, then to a state highway patrol officer who transported him to Grand Marais. He was brought into the law enforcement center and turned over to officers, then put in a cell while authorities from his community were notified. I was dispatching the afternoon this person was brought in.

Seeing as he had so much contact with other law enforcement agencies, I figured he had been searched. During this time period we put prisoners in jail in their street clothes. Early the next morning, when the city clerk came to work, he went back to check on this teen and another prisoner we were holding on a felony charge. The teen had a pistol stuck in his boot and forced the city employee to unlock the cell at gunpoint. When he was let out of his cell, the teen let the other prisoner out and they fled on foot. The police chief called me at home and asked me some questions regarding this prisoner. I told him since he had gone through so many law enforcement agencies, a weapon should have been discovered. Guess not! I did feel somewhat guilty about it, but I didn't think it was a dispatcher's responsibility.

Later that day, my dad and I were hauling garbage to the dump located on the road past the Scenic Overlook, a couple of miles up the Gunflint Trail from Grand Marais. This dump had a cliff on the northwest side as you drove in. This is the area where one dumped their garbage. On the right side was a sloping, wooded area that went back down the hill toward Highway 61. It offered a panoramic view of Lake Superior. While we were getting rid of our garbage, two males came out of the woods from down below and walked toward us. I recognized them as the escapees and told my dad. He had his .45 semi-automatic pistol with him and when they got closer he drew his weapon on them. The teen went to his waist for his weapon, but my dad told him what would happen if he produced a gun. He wisely raised his arms, and we took them both back to jail. I felt somewhat vindicated. Thank goodness my dad had his gun that day. As with any job, some days were busier than others. This was certainly one of the more memorable ones.

I have fond memories of the year and a half I dispatched. The quiet shifts around 3:00 am, I would walk to the front door, step out and hear the waves rolling in and just drink in the quiet of the night. On some nights Nona, a local woman who cleaned the lounge next to the police station, would bring me a bag or two of popcorn. The things one remembers.

A significant event took place in the summer of 1972. My former boss resigned from his position as sheriff. Several men tossed their hats in the ring as the county board was going to appoint a new candidate to fill the term. John, the African American part-time deputy in the West End was appointed and suddenly, at least according to the media, Cook County had a novelty. He was the only black sheriff in the state living and working in a northern county with an Indian reservation and an all-white population. I had no intention of working in Cook County at this time and continued waiting for my call to the Border Patrol. I waited until early Spring of 1973 and decided to inquire. I had been told I was on the highly recommended list and I wondered why I hadn't received a call-up. I explained my situation to my local congressman and he placed a couple of calls. Shortly thereafter, I received a letter from him stating that the Department of Immigration informed him that apparently two Richard Dorrs had taken the test and had scored the identical score. That seemed unbelievable to me. As far as I know, no Richard Dorr was ever called to the Border Patrol. I figured I got lost in the political shuffle. Now I really regretted letting that Alexandria job get away.

I started job searching and learned of several police openings in departments near the Minneapolis area. One of those was in Elk River, a community west of the cities along Highway 10. I took their test and interview and got the job. I put a $500 deposit on an apartment and got my uniforms and drove back to Grand Marais wondering if this was where I really wanted to go. This decision seemed like a rash one and I ultimately chose not to take the job. I lost my $500 deposit and had to mail back the uniforms.

Grand Marais, being a coastal community on Lake Superior, the largest of the great lakes, had a U.S. Coast Guard station with several men stationed there. That is where Stan, a local police officer, did his military time and met his future wife. Another Coastie, as we called them, also met a local girl and ended up marrying her. Mary was a classmate of mine and when her husband's tour of duty ended, they moved to Marshall, Minnesota where he went to work for the police department. Mary heard I was interested in getting back into law enforcement and one evening when I was dispatching, she called the police department and told me of an opening with the Lyon County Sheriff's Department in Marshall. Mary and her husband were good friends with the sheriff, and they felt my chances would be good if I came down to Marshall and applied for the job. I went home and looked up Marshall on a map. It is in southwestern Minnesota and is flat, farming country.

I talked it over with Laurie and she was excited to go take a look at this opportunity. In the early summer of 1973, Laurie and I drove the 400 miles to Marshall and liked what the town offered. There are several major highways going through this community. It is a fairly short drive to Sioux Falls, South Dakota to the southwest and to Minneapolis to the east. Marshall is a college town with a population close to twelve thousand. There are several small towns in Lyon County, most of them having at least one police officer. Mary and her husband Curly arranged a meeting with the sheriff. That night we met John, the sheriff, and his wife. He was tall and thin, a ramrod straight kind of guy. He had sharp features and I'll always remember the western style boots he was wearing. He was extremely welcoming and made us feel at ease right away. The interview amounted to an evening out with him and his wife. Everywhere we went he was warmly received and it appeared he was a real people person. One reason I was highly considered for the job was that I had already completed BCA training. There was a hospital in Marshall and it didn't appear that Laurie would have trouble finding employment. The Lyon County Sheriff's Department was slowly growing and if hired, I would be the sixth deputy on the department. At the end of our visit, John offered me the job. All we had to do was figure out a starting date. We decided on August 1st, and we planned our move around that date.

Laurie and I returned to Grand Marais with both excitement and the normal apprehension of leaving an area that I had roots in. There were people I was going to miss as I had gotten to know the police officers and state patrolmen so well while working as a dispatcher. Laurie and I had been helped so much by Stan when we were living out in the country and running the cabins. He was a fiercely proud German and when I told him my wife's maiden name was Schmeling, she could do no wrong in his eyes. Our social circle was small, but Laurie had gotten close to the wife of one of the new border patrolmen. We also spent quite a bit of time in the West End getting to know Dan, the new warden. Laurie also developed a friendship with his wife, Gail. One of our favorite things to do with them was to drive to Duluth and have dinner at the Chinese Lantern, a very popular dining destination. The prime rib there could feed a family, but Dan could eat it all.

Another man I liked was Don, a highway patrol officer. I had an opportunity to ride patrol with Don shortly before we moved, and I came to know the man and some of his thoughts. Based on conversations we shared, there were other courses in life he wished he had pursued, much like I discovered later in my career.

I'd miss Joe, the police chief, too. It took a lot of courage to change careers in midlife as he had done. As I was leaving in 1973, he had only been an officer in Grand Marais for seven years and was still learning the job. He enjoyed fishing and golf among other things, and we had some good times together.

Prior to leaving, I stopped up at the courthouse and spoke with John, the new sheriff. His office was still in the basement of the courthouse, and he was busy learning his new job and how to organize things. In my opinion, knowing John, he would incorporate evening patrols into his schedule. I remember thinking he had a lot of organizing to do and deputies to hire. As a dispatcher, I observed the growing pains the Grand Marais Police Department had experienced and I didn't envy the job facing the new sheriff.

August 1st was soon approaching so we loaded up the truck and headed out. As Laurie and I drove out of town and up the long hill that takes you west out of Grand Marais, I couldn't help but look in the rearview mirror and take in the sight of the town I loved. I don't think I realized how much this meant until we crested the hill and it was no more.

5

GOOD TIMES AND BAD TIMES

Laurie was looking forward to our move to Marshall and everything it offered. I took it for granted that everyone felt the same way about Grand Marais that I did. I think what Laurie was going to miss the most, other than some good friends, were my parents. She was not going to miss the isolation of living far from shopping opportunities and other creature comforts. It was more important to her to live much closer to her family. We would be only ninety miles away and we would have more opportunities to see them.

Laurie and I had lived in simple living quarters from our first apartment in Grand Marais, to our one-bedroom apartment in Ely, to the simple little house we had on the lower Croftville road in Grand Marais. We were just content to have a decent roof overhead.

When we arrived in Marshall, one thing became very clear to me. The temperature! There is no fair way to compare 65 degrees by the lake versus 95 degrees with 90 percent humidity. That would be one of my biggest obstacles. I think Laurie kind of chuckled to herself about that. Continuing our modest living style, we rented a double-wide mobile home in a park just south of Marshall-328 Timberlane Drive. Unlike Grand Marais, there were plenty of rentals available from houses to apartments, but we chose to spend our first year in this mobile home.

Everything about Marshall seemed a good fit. It was a good-sized community with lots of shopping and recreation. I enjoyed a completely new professional approach to my job. My new boss had leadership qualities that made the job rewarding. The fact that there was a chief deputy and four other road officers meant I wasn't going to be the primary responder like I had been in Cook County. I also wasn't going to know everyone I was dealing with.

The way Lyon County was laid out was entirely new to me. This was flat, farming country that was actually sectioned off with roads every mile. There were roads running east and west and those running north and south. That may sound funny, but you cannot appreciate that scenario unless you have worked in an area like Cook County. It took me a while to get used to the land itself. I wasn't used to seeing lights far off in the distance while patrolling at night. One could see for miles. The wooded terrain I came from was mountainous and rocky and roads followed high country ridges. Most country roads in Cook County were tree lined and that is all you could see. In my new surroundings I was in a much smaller county with more miles of drivable roads and wide-open fields.

The small towns throughout the county usually had at least one officer and while on patrol I got to know them and the people in their communities. I was made aware that buildings on farm sites could be targets for burglars in the spring of the year due to agrochemicals stored in them. Anhydrous ammonia for instance, can be used in the production of methamphetamine. Criminals were always passing through the major highways going through this community. With a college of several thousand students, there were the adventures they brought to the job, especially on the weekends. With more people to serve, there was more civil process, domestic incidents, car accidents and other police related activities. There was much less water activity, however.

I was the sixth deputy hired in this growing department. The Marshall Police Department had at least twice as many men as the sheriff's department but there was a spirit of cooperation between the departments. Both departments had their own buildings and dispatchers. The police department was downtown, and the sheriff's department was near the courthouse in the western edge of the community. Our building was an old brick, two-story house remodeled to accommodate the sheriff's department. Downstairs we had a kitchen, jail, dispatch area, and offices for the sheriff and the deputies. There was an upstairs level with a bathroom and other rooms that eventually came into use as the department grew.

My first evening on the job, I rode with a deputy named Lee. He was a local man, and he was good at not swamping me with too much information right away. I was 26 and he was a couple of years younger. Everything was new to me, and I absorbed as much as I could. I was in an organized department and could start to relate to the conversations of my friends from BCA school. After riding with Lee for a few days, I started to feel more acquainted with the area and I could actually find my way back to Marshall from the most remote area of the county. Lee and I seemed to have a lot in common and we discovered so did our wives. Carol, his wife, worked at a local bank and Laurie had no trouble finding work at the hospital. As couples we socialized and developed a close friendship.

The call of the sheriff's department was 100. The sheriff was 101. Don, our chief deputy and investigator was 102 and then down the line as seniority followed. I was 106. The other officers on the department were all welcoming. Denny, number 103, had grown up in this part of the state and was the deputy canine officer. Syn was his German Shepard and rather than call him an attack dog, let's say he was a peace-keeper and very loyal to his partner. Then there was Jim, number 104, a hard charging adventurous type of guy and Doug, number 105, a baby-faced new hire who hadn't been on the department much longer than me.

The day shift usually started with the sheriff and the deputies on duty meeting at the Happy Chef restaurant. During coffee we decided on our patrol duties for the day. This sheriff, who had been a Marshall police officer prior to becoming sheriff, had a unique way of being one of the guys yet always leaving no doubt who was in charge.

This was an era where the sheriff's department prepared meals for the prisoners. Usually, the deputies working the day shift took care of breakfast and lunch and the sheriff's wife prepared the evening meal. So, in the morning we would feed the prisoners, find out if there were papers to serve or complaints to follow up on from the previous shift, go out for coffee and then hit the road. As I became more familiar with the county, I felt at ease in getting to know the people I encountered.

With August under my belt and a growing friendship with Lee and his wife, I asked him if they wanted to take a short trip up to Grand Marais and visit the area I came from. We both liked to hunt so in mid-September 1973, we decided to do some grouse hunting in Cook County. I felt a warm feeling as Lake Superior came into view. We stayed on the lower Croftville Road and took day trips into the backcoun-try. It was a good trip, and I touched bases with some of the officers and shared some details of my new job.

When we returned to Marshall, I discovered a new love. Lee introduced me to pheasant hunting. We didn't have dogs yet, but there were some small sloughs we could walk and kick up enough birds to have for supper. It was great!

My parents visited our humble home in October. My dad had retired from the Border Patrol in 1972 and when Laurie and I moved, they chose to relocate closer to some of their old friends and my dad's brother, Cliff. They decided to have a home built for them in their hometown of Chippewa Falls, Wisconsin. We had a good visit, but I sensed dad never really liked Marshall. He didn't feel comfortable with the way the city was laid out. I think what really bothered him was knowing we were in flat, tornado country.

The day after my folks left, I got a phone call that would change forever the way I would look upon Grand Marais. The law enforcement center called and told me that Don, the trooper I had visited with on our trip with Lee and Carol, was shot and killed during a routine traffic stop. The word 'routine' didn't seem appropriate in that phrase anymore. He had stopped a vehicle and was in the process of dealing with the female driver who had been drinking when her husband became argumentative and retrieved a weapon from the vehicle. He began shooting into the windshield of the squad car and, when Don exited the squad car, he was struck down by gunfire. The man then approached Don, took his service revolver and shot the fallen officer before turning the gun on himself, committing suicide. I was stunned. Nothing ever prepares you for that kind of news. You always hear about that happening somewhere else, not in your hometown and certainly not to someone you know. That was the third homicide in Cook County in three years and for me, the most painful. An incident like that takes away the innocence of an area forever. I went out onto my back porch and wept. The next few days were tough. My boss permitted me to drive a squad car to Grand Marais and be part of the law enforcement presence at the funeral. Seeing all the officers present at full attention was one of the most impressive and emotional experiences I've ever had. All the way back to Marshall I kept thinking about the conversations I had with this man just months prior and it all seemed surreal.

November and December went by, and I continued to learn about my new area and fellow officers. I was well received by the small-town officers and the Marshall police officers. Things were going along well and then the BCA notified my boss that upon reviewing certifications of officers on departments, they discovered prior to my being hired in Lyon County, I had been out of law enforcement more than one year and would probably need to go through BCA school again. Since my first school, the hours of the training sessions had increased from 175 to 280. So, what my boss thought was a bargain when I was hired, turned out to be an unexpected expense as he was also sending Doug to this training session.

On January 28, 1974, Doug and I went to Minneapolis for BCA school that would take us through March 22. There were 44 other officers at this class, two were women. The instructors from the BCA were the same instructors from my first class. Of course, they had not forgotten that I shot up the motel in Alexandria in 1970. I told Doug about that prior to the class because I knew it would come up in conversation. Some of the courses were redundant but my test scores were good, and the additional training was a benefit. I returned to Marshall fully certified. At this class, I came in second in the shooting event by one point to a hotshot cop from Burnsville, Minnesota. I had to give the guy credit because he was firing a .38 caliber revolver with a two-inch barrel which is more difficult to be accurate with from the distances we fired from.

The most exciting thing that happened to me was a phone call I received from my wife one evening. She was pregnant.

What an amazing feeling that was! I couldn't wait to get back home and see her.

After my return, Laurie and I decided to look for another place to live. We found a large farmhouse for rent a couple miles north of Marshall and decided to move into the country. Interestingly enough, another farmhouse was available across the section from us and Lee and Carol rented that. It turned out that Carol was pregnant too. Lee and I both got Golden Retriever hunting dogs from the same litter. Our lives seemed to be following a similar path. Our home was a two-story farmhouse with large rooms. In the basement, there was a large circular cistern over six feet tall that contained the water supply for the home.

Spring and summer were wonderful in farm country. When the snow melted, the grass was actually green. The genuinely warm spring days are one thing I recall with fondness about farm country.

In May 1974, I was sent to radar certification classes and that was added to my resume of qualifications. I was quite nervous the first time I stopped a car and approached a citizen who had been speeding. I thought it fascinating the more folks I stopped for speeding, the more interesting their stories or excuses got. I chased after one fellow who would not stop, and I ended up following him into his yard in the country. He ran for the house and as I exited my squad, he hollered, "Just leave the ticket on the dash, I've got to go to the bathroom!" Another time I stopped a car full of nuns. I gave them a warning and as I started back to my vehicle, one of them rolled down the rear window and said, "Bless you son". I felt pretty safe the rest of the day.

Living in a more populated area did bring some strangeness to our lives. While Laurie was pregnant and still working, she apparently was being observed by some pervert who stalked pregnant women. We started getting nasty phone calls and one evening, someone followed Laurie home from work and came up our driveway which was about two blocks long. A vehicle with no lights on stopped in front of the house and Laurie came in and laughingly said that she thought one of the officers in the area was playing a joke on us. I went to the front yard and when the driver in this vehicle saw me, he peeled backwards out of the driveway before I could get dressed and give chase. The nonsense seemed to end after our baby was born but it bothered me that we never identified this guy.

Summer rolled along and Laurie and I found ourselves enjoying this area more and more. Laurie's friendships with other officers' wives developed into a solid base that made Marshall feel like home. August 22nd marked the arrival of our firstborn, a son we named Mitchell. When the time comes, you go to the hospital for the delivery and then you go home with this new little package. It's yours to keep! I was a dad! There are no words to describe the feeling. Being a daddy and learning about country living filled my plate that summer.

Life was good and we were enjoying our country setting. There was an established asparagus patch where the farm fields met our grove of trees. That was my first introduction to this vegetable. I tried my hand at a little gardening and grew some carrots and potatoes. You could actually dig your shovel in the rich soil and not hit a rock unlike the rocky, clay soil up North. Laurie was having fun with our little son, and it wasn't too much later that Lee and Carol had their baby, a little girl named Jodi. She was Mitch's first playmate. Our little neighborhood in the country was getting busy. Lee and I had been working with our Golden Retrievers. Lee called his dog "Buster", I called my dog "Ladd". One of my joys in this part of the state was pheasant hunting. Most of the time a dog was needed so they were added to the family.

Fall season turned to winter and we spent Christmas at Laurie's parents' home. She came from a large family and her siblings all stayed close to their home area. Laurie's two brothers had newborn boys as well, so Christmas was very special that year. Of course, babies always get attention, and Mitchell joined his two new cousins sitting on their Grandpa Schmeling's lap. My parents who were in Chippewa Falls, Wisconsin had Christmas with my dad's brother, Cliff, and their mother.

Back home in Marshall in the early part of January 1975, we had no idea what was in store for us. On January 12th, a blizzard hit the area unlike anything I had ever seen. I'd never experienced a winter storm in prairie country before and wasn't prepared. The old farmhouse creaked and groaned as the wind blew. The thick snow came down so hard that you could not see anything in front of you. It struck so fast. We weren't going to venture out with our baby until it broke. That was two days later. We were stranded. Wherever there was a building or grove of trees, snow had drifted into massive hills. Our well and pump disappeared under the snow, the car was buried, and we couldn't open any doors on the main level of the house to get out. There was one miracle that took place. We never lost our power so we were able to have heat. I was convinced that would be my last winter in the country. Unlike the farmers in the area, I didn't have the equipment to deal with this type of snow. That storm became known as the blizzard of the century and some folks who were stranded in their vehicles didn't make out so well.

That winter finally came to an end followed by typical beautiful Spring weather. Early April of 1975 turned into a sad time for our family. I was home for lunch and took a phone call from one of Laurie's brothers. He notified us that Laurie's father, Ernest, had passed away from a heart attack at age 58. I had known this man just five years and he was a generous, loving father. Laurie was really close to her dad, so this news hit her hard. April 9th found us in Cosmos with the rest of the family for the funeral. What made this especially difficult was that he had three new grandsons. As we go along in life, nature has a way of letting us know that with the good times come the bad times. We returned home to our farmsite and in May, my folks came for a visit. My parents thought the world of Laurie and I know my dad wanted her to feel more like a daughter than a daughter-in-law.

I was constantly introduced to new situations. This community differed from my old one. There were large commercial retail stores both in town and on the outer edges, an industrial park with many small thriving businesses and Schwann's, a worldwide-renowned ice cream manufacturing plant. There was a large Turkey Valley Farms turkey processing plant, three dance halls in the county, two state parks and the college. Throw into that mix the farmers, elevators and other farm-related industries. There were miles of state and county roads to patrol and there was a lot to do. We wore western style deputy hats that we had to have on when we got out of our squad. The sheriff said they made us four inches taller and that would be a psychological advantage. Given that reasoning, I guess I went from 6'4" to 6'8".

Several of the larger stores on the outskirts of town kept caged dogs outside their buildings at night. Alarms were wired in to our office and when the dispatcher heard a dog barking at a particular location, we'd check it out. One night I responded to a hardware store after such an alarm and found a door open. It was creepy entering the building feeling like a sitting duck. I was trained that the best weapon in the dark was the good old 12-gauge shotgun with 00 buck. As I cautiously walked through the store, I was not sure I would find anything or not and in retrospect, that represents letting your guard down mentally. A lesson I would soon learn. As I neared the manager's office, I still had not discovered anything suspicious. Slowly going around a corner, I suddenly came face to face with a man aiming a gun at me. Just as I was thinking about pulling the trigger, I realized this was a wall mirror and I was looking at myself. You had to be there to appreciate that scenario. The store was clear, and it turned out that one of the employees had forgotten to lock up.

Civil process serving was also challenging. There were so many different types of papers to serve and some people were quite evasive. On more than one occasion we were asked to serve papers on employees at Turkey Valley Farms. We always contacted the business office before going into this facility and they would escort the employee into a private room. We didn't want to cause them embarrassment. This plant was a real eye opener for me. I'd never seen so many dead birds before, and the smell was something to behold.

I learned one of the best lessons of my life while serving papers. One evening, I had an order to remove a man from his home after he and his wife had been involved in a nasty domestic incident. He was in the process of making court appearances after being charged with assault. This particular order was to remove him from the home. It was pre-arranged that the wife would not be present when this paper was served. I knew the man somewhat from prior contacts and didn't anticipate a problem. He was a construction worker. I knocked on the door and was admitted by him into the home. I informed him why I was there, and he agreed to leave. He gave me a cup of coffee and asked if he could throw some clothes together. I told him to go ahead and sat down at the kitchen table. I had only taken my eyes off the hallway he had gone down for a second when I heard the ratchet of the slide action of a gun. I looked up and at the same time reached for my pistol. He came around the hall corner with a shotgun in his hand and said "I suppose I can't take this with me." He chose a poor time to state the obvious and he worked the slide to show it was empty. He could have just as easily tried to take me out. Instructors talk about things like that in school, but the point really hits home when that happens to you out in the field. Incidents like this make it difficult for the public to understand some of our reactions in certain situations. I decided right then and there that if I wanted to keep coming home to my wife and son, I'd better get my head out of my ass!

Those situations were unpredictable but, they were part of the job. Things back in Grand Marais were not going so well for the police department. Joe, the chief, had been battling cancer, a battle he lost in April of 1975. While he was still able to work, one of the part time officers was lobbying hard to get his job. This created tension for Stan, the full-time officer who naturally felt he should be the next chief. When

Joe passed away, Stan did get the chief's position, and I was glad for him. He hired a local man who was a lifelong resident of Grand Marais. Jim was a good man, but he would learn soon enough the stresses of working in your home community.

Meanwhile, I had more educational opportunities for my job. I went to a report writing class and a courtroom demeanor seminar that involved testimony presentation. Also, in July of '75, another deputy and I were sent to St. Cloud to participate in a pursuit driving class. Our squad cars were Plymouths with a lot of horsepower and were very fast. We spent a couple of days finding out the limits of these cars. I came back to the community itching to get in a chase. That was one thing we never had to wait long to do. The roads were so long and straight and it wasn't uncommon to meet drivers going very fast. I think the fastest person I clocked on radar was going 108 mph. When someone is going that fast and you have to stop and turn around to pursue them, they end up with a good head start. Our department also worked with other jurisdictions doing blood runs across this part of the state for a patient that may need a rare type.

Our little boy was soon going to be one year old, and I didn't want to go through the possibility of another blizzard in the country. Laurie and I found a cute little two-bedroom house just two blocks from the sheriff's office. We ended up buying it for a whopping $17,500. We moved in August and became first-time homeowners. Once again, we kept it modest. We had a nice lot that was quite generous. Having a baby, I fenced in the yard with a chain link fence that, I believe, is still standing. We had a small garage out back and a garden plot and life was good. We had a child, good jobs, nice friends and a great town to live in. One thought kept nagging at me though. Whenever we'd make periodic trips back North or I would be parked out in the countryside near one of the small neighboring towns, my thoughts would drift towards returning to Grand Marais someday. I didn't have a clue when that might be, but the thought was always there. Of course, I had to weigh those feelings against the way my wife felt. She loved this rural community and what it offered. She was very happy to be so much closer to her family. But who knew what the future would hold?

Lyon County Sherriff's Department

6

KEEPING BUSY

The town of Marshall was very supportive of law enforcement. Every Christmas, local businesses would fill the sheriff's trunk with items for the officers. There would be sets of steak knives, turkeys, 12-packs of beer, bottles of booze and other goodies. It was a little something for all the false alarms we answered and the eye we kept on their businesses. We felt appreciated and those gestures never compromised our actions as officers. Gifts today would be questioned as unethical.

I've mentioned earlier that there were several towns in our patrol area in Lyon County. Cottonwood was north of Marshall on Highway 23 and had a police chief. Ghent, Minneota, and Taunton were northwest of Marshall along Highway 68 and were spaced about 6 miles from each other. Minneota had a police chief. Ghent had a ballroom that was popular with college students, particularly when the legislature, in their infinite wisdom, lowered the drinking age to eighteen. Because of the ballroom's increased activity,

Ghent hired an officer. Lynd and Russell were southwest of Marshall along Highway 23, and they were small communities that contracted with the sheriff's department for law enforcement services. Russell eventually hired an officer for their community. Lynd also had a ballroom that was very busy on weekends. Highway 59 ran south of Marshall and intersected with Highway 14, a state highway that ran east and west through the lower end of our county. The towns of Balaton and Tracy were located along Highway 14 and had hired officers.

All the highways going through this county presented opportunities for the criminal element to pay us visits. One early morning, I and a fellow deputy had just finished our shift and were at the Happy Chef restaurant after 0100am. We saw a Marshall squad car heading east at a high rate of speed and learned they were responding to an alarm at a retail recreation store on the outskirts of town just across Highway 23 from the college. We responded to back them up and ended up partially foiling a burglary in progress. Burglars had come into town from north Highway 23, parked in the college parking lot among all the other vehicles and walked through the cornfields that were growing all around this store. They entered the building through the roof and inadvertently triggered a motion sensor. They had a spotter and were out of the building as officers arrived. As they made their way through the cornfield to where their vehicle was parked, they were dropping items as they ran in the dark. By the time the store was secured and their path out was discovered, they got away. At least for that night. Marshall investigators eventually linked them to Duluth. This would be a group of thieves I would encounter later in my career.

The first summer I worked in Lyon County, I was called to a motor vehicle accident on a winding, black-topped road called the Skunk Hollow Road. A young male college student crashed his vehicle off this road and was thrown in the back seat. He died before my eyes as I was trying to get the car door open. This young man turned out to be from Silver Bay, Minnesota, a community just west of Grand Marais along the North Shore. How strange it was that both the attempted burglary and the fatal accident occurred within blocks of each other and involved people from the area I came from.

Between work and family activities, time flew by. Mitchell had his first birthday in our new home, and we took autumn trips to see Laurie's family and visit my parents at their new home in Wisconsin. Winter went quickly, if that's ever possible, and 1976 turned into a very big year. Laurie has a younger sister, Chellie, who shares the same birthday, and they have a special bond. In 1976, Laurie was 26 and Chellie was 18. Chellie was getting married, and her two sisters were going to be part of the ceremony. The wedding was to be in July and provided for some exciting summer planning between Chellie, Laurie and Lornette, their older sister. One of the advantages of living in Marshall was that Laurie could just scoot over to Cosmos in an hour and a half. July finally came and the wedding went off without a hitch. Laurie has a nice singing voice and sang at her sister's wedding which made it all the more special. Shortly after the wedding, we made a short trip to Grand Marais. This time I stopped at the sheriff's office and inquired about future job opportunities. I indicated an interest to Sheriff Lyght and got my name on a list.

I continued to be exposed to new calls and had many career learning experiences on the job. I responded to a suicide call, the second of my career. In this case the cause of death was by hanging. I found that type of call to be the ultimate mystery. At this point in my life, I tried to understand the misery or desperation, or courage it took for that type of action. I also was part of a roadblock situation that involved a high-speed chase heading our way from the Iowa border.

The pursuit involved a state trooper following a stolen car. The sheriff directed that a roadblock be set up a few miles south of Marshall on Highway 59. As I set up at the rear end of the blockade, the sheriff instructed me that this vehicle was not to get past us and into town. If this vehicle got as far as me, I was to use any means to stop it. I remember taking out the shotgun and hoping they got the car stopped before it got to me. I knew what "any means possible" involved. Thankfully, they did run the car off the road and stopped the pursuit with no injuries.

In July, I had an opportunity to fall back on a little of my knowledge of Border Patrol and immigration law. Shortly before 0100am on a warm summer morning, I was dispatched to Liberty Park in downtown Marshall. A woman had been mugged, and her purse had been stolen. Two suspects fled the scene and I and three Marshall police officers located the suspects hiding in the bushes of a drainage ditch that ran through this park. When ordered, they wouldn't come out. The Marshall police, with the assistance of their police dog, flushed the men out of the ditch. I and another officer went in the ditch and found the stolen purse. We never had any physical contact with the men, one of whom was Hispanic and claimed not to speak English. I figured that was the end of it. However, a few days later, I'm being named in a potential suit as one of the officers who used unnecessary force against this Hispanic individual. Apparently, the police canine nipped the Hispanic man in the rear end while flushing him and the other suspect from the ditch. The State Human Rights Department got involved and, without doing any research, blanketed us all as defendants in a civil action. I suspected this Hispanic man was an illegal alien so I called immigration authorities. They came and verified that he was in the country illegally. He was deported back to Mexico. End of suit. This typical bleeding-heart crap from some of these agencies contributed to some of my early layers of cynicism.

Another early morning call came to a rare conclusion. The actual apprehension of a burglar inside a building! After a silent alarm in a Tracy grocery store went off, the Tracy police responded and set up a perimeter around the building. The police had a suspect in custody and had identified a vehicle parked about a block away that they felt was involved in this incident. The car had all kinds of meat products in it, and it seemed obvious that the amount of loot in the car indicated more than one person must be involved. I and another deputy responded and asked the subject in custody if there was anyone else in the store. Of course, he said there was no one else involved. While the police maintained the secure perimeter outside, my partner and I went in and started to grid search the store. This differed from other store searches as I was damn sure there were unknown suspects in this building. Not knowing if they were armed or not, we slowly worked our way up the aisles with flashlights and shotguns. About halfway up the third aisle in my section of the store, I was panning my flashlight over the lower shelf of soap displays when the beam of my light lit up a human face. I placed the muzzle of my shotgun on his forehead and told him to slowly roll out into the aisle. My adrenalin was really pumping because I realized that no matter how ready I was, if he had a weapon, things could have gotten ugly. We cleared the rest of the store. These were the only two men involved. In their possession they had their casing book that noted similar type grocery stores that they were hitting from Sioux Falls, South Dakota to Minneapolis. They told us the Tracy store wasn't on their list but it looked like a sitting duck so they had to hit it. Guess they should have passed on it.

The summer and autumn of 1976 sailed by and it wasn't long before we were celebrating our second Christmas in our small two-bedroom home on Saratoga Street. Little did I know what the new year would bring.

We made a Christmas trip over to Cosmos to celebrate the holiday with Laurie's family and another trip in January for Laurie's birthday. In February, I received a call from John Lyght, the sheriff in Cook County. He was going to have an opening for a deputy in the very near future and wanted to know if I was interested. Now it was decision time! As I look back on the decisions I made in my life, they all seemed about ME! Laurie married me and took my name. She converted to my religion. She followed me to Ely and supported me when I went to school. She gave me a child. And now, I was about to ask her if she would once again return to Grand Marais, a remote, northern location far away from her family so I could pursue my career ambitions once again. How do you measure the depth of a person's loving support?

When we talked about this new job opportunity, she agreed to give it a try. She knew how much I missed Lake Superior, the woods, and surrounding areas and was going to let me follow my dream. I returned the sheriff's call and asked him if he could send me a job offer in writing to show my boss in Marshall. A short time later I received his letter. At that point, Laurie and I started getting things in order and putting our house up for sale.

7

RETURNING TO GRAND MARAIS

The officers in Lyon County gave us a nice farewell party at the Legion Hall in downtown Marshall. I don't think I've ever been closer to a group of people. It seems hard to believe one could develop bonds like that in less than four years. Denny Rokeh, a police officer in Russell, and his wife Martha helped us make the move. Typical of Grand Marais, there wasn't much available for sale or rent at this time. Nevertheless, we arrived in Grand Marais on April 1, 1977, and moved into a small cabin in an alley in the middle of town. I was back in the community I grew up in. I can still remember the day we hit town. April on the North Shore was cold, a stark contrast to southwestern Minnesota. There was no one there to greet us and I recall having my doubts about this move. The cabin had a small basement to house what we couldn't fit in the upstairs living quarters.

A Grand Marais spring is usually just flat-out crappy. Ice is usually still on the inland lakes, the breezes off Lake Superior are downright frigid and several of the seasonal shops aren't even open yet. While Laurie tried to make our cracker box a home, I familiarized myself with the sheriff's department. Little did I know how much the area had changed and how much law enforcement needed to grow.

The working environment had changed quite a bit. The municipal building downtown had added an addition for a new law enforcement center. The public utilities and law center were now separate buildings. The Grand Marais police and the sheriff were under the same roof. The entry to this building off Broadway Street had been remodeled to access the law enforcement center. This building included the dispatch/record keeping office and offices for the police chief, sheriff and a troop room with several desks for deputies and state troopers. This setting provided for more interaction among officers. In addition, a separate hall from the dispatch area led to a small visitation room for prisoners, a booking room and a hall leading back to the jail. There were three singular cells and a bullpen that could hold five prisoners.

There were two deputies working in Cook County prior to my arrival. They were Larry Dahl, a deputy assigned to Grand Portage, and Dick Stone who had been full time in the department about one year before I arrived and seasonal before that. Two other deputies had left the county and relocated to other departments. That accounted for an officer shortage in our county. I rode with Dick the first few days and he brought me up to date about new changes and people in the county. There were definitely some new characters to learn about since I last worked here in 1971. Some not so nice characters I might add.

The Cook County sheriff was in the process of trying to grow his department to catch up with the times. It seemed to me he couldn't do this fast enough. Cook County was a much larger area than the farming county I came from and there weren't enough deputies for adequate coverage. The department hadn't heard of unions yet and the deputies were working incredible hours without overtime compensation. I learned from fellow deputies, the sheriff, and the Grand Marais police officers about some of the problem areas and people to watch. There were dopers, burglars, thieves, and a group of local men who would fit into all of those categories. There were also significant criminal sexual misconduct investigations going on. Let's just say I hit the ground running. Compared to where I had been working, this seemed like the Wild West. Cook County was part of the state being discovered by more and more people and as it became more exposed, so did its problems.

In early May, the sheriff sent me to the Minneapolis area for an 80-hour evidence collection school. It was a good school, but it always served to remind me of our lack of resources in the remote jurisdiction we worked in. The BCA would be available to assist with more serious cases but, for the most part, we preserved our own crime scenes which included dusting for latent fingerprints, taking photos, collecting evidence and interviewing witnesses. Just because I worked for a small department, I didn't want to be considered a less skilled officer so I always appreciated any schooling.

I was fortunate to have some good mentors along the way. One I met in 1977 was the Cook County attorney, Richard Swanson. He had been the assistant Dean of the School of Law at the University of Minnesota. His friends in the cities all thought he was making a mistake to move to the North Shore and give up a legal practice in the cities. It was my good fortune to have the opportunity to learn from him. We certainly did not always agree but logical arguing was a strength of his and we shared our different viewpoints respectfully.

When June rolled around, the department hired two more officers-Ken Carlson and Margee Plum. Ken went on the road full time after originally being hired as a part-time deputy. Margee started out as a seasonal campground deputy, and she was utilized in the back country. She went on many stakeouts with us.

The summer of 1977 was busy. There were two criminal sexual misconduct (crim-sex) cases being investigated prior to my arrival. The first case involved a camp counselor operating a youth camp halfway up the Gunflint Trail on an area lake. He was charged with six counts of crim-sex abuse and convicted in July of 1977. The victims were all young males. The case wasn't discovered until one of the young males returned home for the summer and informed his father about what took place. The boy's father was a lawyer and notified Cook County authorities. The camp counselor pled guilty, was placed on a 30-year probation and ordered out of Cook County. People involved felt the sentence was a joke.

The other case involved a school official and formal charges were dropped due to the sensitive nature of involving young children whose parents wouldn't permit them to testify.

There were five auto thefts, three drownings, multiple vehicle break-ins, two fatal car accidents and seven burglaries, one of which was a safe job. It's difficult to adequately describe the hours these incidents took to investigate, and it wasn't as if patrol duties, paper service and other calls could be neglected.

The vehicle break-ins were being committed by a group of local men who made it their mission to break into parked vehicles and steal belongings from people who were out on canoe trips. Most of these break-ins occurred to vehicles in remote wooded areas far from Grand Marais which provided the thieves with some security. Round Lake, Brule Lake, Eagle Mountain and Flour Lake were popular locations. Even the addition of two deputies to make four made it difficult to catch these guys. We spent hours on stakeouts that eventually would result in going home tired and not making an arrest.

In June, a school bus that had been converted into a camper lost its brakes coming down the Gunflint Trail. There was a family of nine on board. They shot across Highway 61, went past the fish houses on the harbor below the highway and into Lake Superior. When I arrived all nine people were standing on the roof of the bus which had totally submerged. It looked like nine people walking on water! What could have been a terrible accident would turn into an amusing situation, from my perspective anyway. Happy ending.

Toward the end of August, while returning from the Gunflint Trail on a parking area stakeout, I observed a vehicle driving around town during early morning hours. It looked like an International Scout with the top removed. I was familiar with the person who owned it. I went to the office to sign off and the phone rang. A caller was reporting a vehicle off the Little Devil Track corner up the Gunflint Trail about three miles from town. The weather was like a London night- cool, damp and lots of fog. I responded to the location. The vehicle I had observed earlier had gone off the road and rolled down a very steep ravine. There were two people in this vehicle. One of these young men died at the scene and the other survived. The corner at Little Devil Track River is notorious for getting fogged in and is difficult to negotiate. These were local young men who were known in the community.

Another tragedy was a double drowning in September of 1977. Two brothers who were taking over Naniboujou Lodge were shooting the rapids in Brule River close to the lodge. This lodge is located 13 miles east of Grand Marais on the Lake Superior side of Highway 61. One brother had a life jacket on, the other did not. There had been heavy rainfalls, and the river was running very fast. The young men had run the rapids several times but, on what happened to be their last run, the raging river overturned their canoe, and they were washed out into Lake Superior. These were men I had gone to school with. We found the brother who was wearing the life jacket right away. He did not survive the rugged entry into the lake. The other brother was not found until several months later when a northeaster storm put his body up on the shore just east of Hovland. That location was several miles east of where he went into the lake. The cases that involved locals were always the most difficult. Not only does one have to deal with the victims, but their grieving families as well.

Some of the thefts and burglaries that occurred in Grand Marais were committed by criminals from outside our area. There was a group of burglars from Duluth that would come up the North Shore every spring and break into businesses and homes that were sitting empty. Stan, the police chief, requested the stores install alarms in their buildings. This turned out to be a good move and after a few years that kind of activity in town slowed down. Once word got out amongst the thieves that there were alarms in area businesses, it made them reluctant to come all the way up the North Shore and ply their trade. The fact that there was only one highway out of town also limited their escape.

As 1977 came to a close, it seemed amazing to me how much had taken place in the few months since our return. We were still in our little cabin, but we were hopeful of finding another place to live in the near future.

8

CHANGING TIMES

I f you had lived in this northern community, one could
sense a change in the political climate. A hot button topic
was Boundary Waters Canoe Area (BWCA) legislation
and what was going to be permitted or not permitted in the
national forest. Were motors going to be outlawed? How
many people would be allowed to use the forest? If permits
were going to be issued, how would that process work? Future
legislation would also limit motor sizes on certain lakes and
outlaw them altogether on a vast tract of the Superior National
Forest. We would see lodges removed that had been in place
for many years. Businesses would be bought out by the government and the face of the forest would be changing. Needless
to say, the old locals who grew up here and made their living
from the forest thought this was a crock! The town of Grand
Marais was the site of protests against the proposed changes.
The first protest was going to take place in April 1978.

In addition to the potential for civil unrest, our department didn't have to wait long for the inevitable calls for
assistance. One of the more unusual calls came in March. My
boss called from the office and asked if I wanted to go on a

"safari". "A what!", I replied. I asked him to repeat the question and once again he asked if I wanted to go on a safari. I said, "Would you please explain what the heck you are talking about?" He informed me that a man who lived on Caribou Lake in the Lutsen area had a full-grown male African lion as a pet and the man's wife had called and reported the lion had destroyed his cage and was loose. Her husband wasn't home, and she wanted the lion killed. I agreed to meet my boss at the office and grabbed my .30 .30 Winchester, the only rifle I had available.

When I arrived at the office, Jim Dols, a state trooper, agreed to join us. I was familiar with the area we were responding to and knew the home was situated along the shore of Caribou Lake a few miles up the Caribou Trail. In March, there were still cross-country skiers using this lake and they could easily ski right past this home. As we headed for Lutsen, at least a 25 mile drive, I hated the thought of what could happen if this lion saw a skier going by. How would the lion react? The drive out was very tense. It was at least 45 minutes from the time of report until we arrived on site.

We entered the yard. We observed Simba, as he was named, standing about fifty yards or so from us with Caribou Lake in the background. It wasn't as though we'd made an elaborate plan on how to deal with this big cat. Slowly, we exited our vehicle with weapons loaded. The three of us decided to aim for an area between his eyes and on a count of three we would all fire. To this day, I can recall how unlike a deer this critter looked as he came into my rifle sights. The fact was, he could be on us in about three strides if he chose to, so I set my shotgun loaded with double buck next to me in case we didn't put him down quickly. I counted to three and three shots went off as one. Simba went down quickly much to our relief. We took a couple pictures and left the animal for the owner to deal with. This really was a large animal, and

I can't even imagine running into that type of beast in the woods. You would probably qualify for the Olympic team trying to ski to safety.

The lion call and the upcoming April protest along with the usual stolen cars and patrol duties were going to make for another busy spring season. Snow was melting and the back country was opening up for travel. A couple of months earlier I had been named chief deputy. Dick, the deputy who was on board when I came back, left the department to go into home construction full time. He was an excellent builder and probably made the right choice for a career change. It was at that point that Ken came on permanently and a fellow named Myron Wilson was hired replacing Larry from Grand Portage.

Just prior to my safari, Laurie and I had been busy looking around the community for a house. There wasn't much available in town, at least not in our price range. We located a smaller, two-bedroom home on West 7th Avenue. It was on a narrow lot but the asking price of $25,000 seemed like a price we could manage. We put down the whopping down payment of $1,000 and financed the balance. We purchased our second home in our married life and kept with our modest theme. It was nothing special, but it was ours and the $178 monthly payments were manageable.

The April protest against the BWCA legislation did take place. Local citizens marched on the US Forestry building and the Grand Marais Utilities turned off the power to the building temporarily. No violence took place, and the protest was mild by today's standards.

A month later, in May, we hired another part-time deputy to work the campgrounds with Margee. His name was Steve Peterson, a big, easy going young man whose father was a conservation officer in Minnesota. The department had increased our personnel by one, so now there were three full-time and two part-time deputies. At the time, we thought that was great. Looking back, it was ridiculous for a county this size to be so understaffed.

Our department had to deal with the fact that 90% of the land in our county was federal or state owned. That being the case, we didn't have a large tax base to draw funding to support the number of officers we would have liked to have on staff. The county commissioners were still coming to grips with changing times and had to take the words of a sheriff with little experience as to what his needs were. I certainly didn't have the knowledge to write a grant, or for that matter, to even know if that would have been an option at this time. Growing pains were all around us. Grand Portage was starting construction on the Radisson Hotel and twenty-five new homes were scheduled to be built in October in their community. In August, the Tofte rescue squad became operational which was wonderful. I was relieved that officers on the high-way and other areas would have that kind of added support. Looking back, it seemed the decision-makers in the county didn't see the changes taking place in full view. The West End had exploded with activity due to all the new families in Taconite Harbor. Grand Portage was going to add a degree of growth with the activity the new Radison Hotel would bring. Throw in the fact of continuing Canadian traffic through the county and increasing tourism, the sheriff's department definitely needed more officers to establish effective night-time patrol duty.

May came with what Stan, the police chief predicted. At least once in the Spring of the year, out-of-town burglars would pay this area a visit. This time, their visit included the safe in the IGA store. In 1978, this store was located downtown on the corner where today's Security State Bank sits. Our department assisted the police whenever we could. I wasn't working on this particular night but learned of the break-in the next day and went to this business with a Grand Marais officer. Thanks to the alarm, the burglars had been spooked out of the store when an officer responded. The officer doing the perimeter check didn't notice a point of entry and there was no more noise over the alarm. The noise from the store ceased so no further action was taken at this time. The dispatcher had called the owner and when he came to work in the morning, he noticed the front door had been forced open and damage to his safe.

The burglars fled before they could finish their mission leaving their tools behind. The tools were very identifiable, especially a hammer with what appeared to be lard on the handle. When I left the store and returned to the office, I checked the dispatch log to see if any unusual license plate inquiries had been called in on the night shift. There was an entry in the dispatch log that a local man had called in with a plate number from a vehicle that had pulled into his driveway early on that morning. We ran the license plate, and it registered to a woman from Duluth. I called the Duluth police and gave them the name of the vehicle owner and they recognized this name immediately. Duluth officers knew the registered owner, a dancer at a local club who ran with some suspected local burglars. I asked if they had mugshots, and they mailed them to our department. I showed the photos to the citizen who called the plate in, and he recognized them as the people in the vehicle. We managed to put potential suspects in our area at the approximate time of the crime.

Next, I inquired from the Duluth police if they knew where these men worked. I was told the last information they had was that my suspects worked for a rendering company in Superior, Wisconsin. In a conversation with our police chief, we knew there were businesses in town that did contract with a rendering company. We surmised that perhaps our burglars might be casing some businesses while they were up here collecting lard. I went to a rendering company in Superior and discovered our suspects had been working there. The supervisor said the men hadn't shown up for work recently and their tools were missing. I showed them the tools I had in my possession, and they identified them as belonging to the business. Remember the guys who visited the retail store down in Marshall and ran through the corn to flee that scene? I found out later these were the same suspects. As it turned out, we didn't get a prosecution. I was told there wasn't enough direct evidence linking them to the store. Even though we didn't have confessions from our suspects, I thought we made a good case for prosecution. However, I'm not the one who has to convince a jury beyond a reasonable doubt. Describing the steps we took in this investigation helps to point out how much time it takes to work on just one case. Each trip to Duluth takes an officer away from his home county for an entire shift. Four hours are wasted just driving. Those are some of the things I never thought we did a good enough job with educating and explaining to the public.

Successful drug busts were always rewarding because they were difficult to achieve in our small, close-knit community. In one case, we had obtained a search warrant for a cabin that was allegedly used in drug trafficking. The sheriff and I and two fellow deputies executed the search warrant on a summer afternoon. The location of this search was a small cabin in the wooded Creechville neighborhood just north of Grand Marais. We approached this cabin and entered. There were three people there, but the object or should I say subject of my attention was a smaller man about 20 years old. He was a motorcycle rider and had been in an accident not long before our visit. He had a full-length leg cast and was using crutches to get around. On the table near him was a pistol, an older model revolver. On the floor next to him was an ice cream bucket that was partially full of chunks of hashish (compressed parts of the cannabis plant typically smoked in a pipe). The hash was in tinfoil and looked ready for sale. We arrested him and left to take him to jail. One thing we forgot to take into consideration was our combined weight. I suppose the four of us came close to 1000 pounds. As we took this suspect out on the little porch of the cabin, it gave way. The four of us jumped off and landed okay but our suspect on crutches took a nasty fall. I guess you had to be there to appreciate it. Sorry for any lack of compassion but all I kept remembering was how much grief guys like this were causing some of our local families.

Myron, one of our new deputies, was a pretty clever guy and it wasn't long before he worked up some information that would result in a very good drug bust. He had put together enough probable cause for a search warrant on a local man's property. It was in a rural area and the quantity of marijuana was substantial, so several officers would assist in the execution of this warrant. This operation was taking place in August and we were waiting for darkness as part of our element of surprise. Of course, that means the search would be later in the evening. Finally, darkness came, and we proceeded to surround the home and outlying area. I and a border patrol agent were quietly working our way toward the rear of the house. I could just feel the excitement as we crept closer. This guy was going to be so surprised. Suddenly, the area around me exploded with noise and the house lights came on. The homeowner was a musher, and I had unknowingly crept into the middle of his sleeping dogs, and they woke up barking. Why they waited until I got in the middle to wake up, I do not know. All I do know is that we lost the element of surprise. To make a long story short, the people in the house had the warrant served on them. We left the residence with customers for jail, twenty-seven pounds of pot and another learning experience.

As far as my personal life went, we actually found time to have visits from family and friends. My dad told me he was upset with me. He said if he'd known I was going to move back, he would never have left. Being a grandfather now, I can relate to how he felt and have often wished he could have spent more time with my sons.

Laurie and I worked on house improvements, and we decided there was enough room in the backyard for a garage. Fred, the part-time West End deputy and Steve, our new man, helped me build one. Fred did all the cement work and the three of us put the garage package together. It turned out very nice. Steve also turned into a fishing buddy and we had some good outings.

Laurie is a nurse by profession but was staying at home for the time being with our son. She shared with me that in January, we'd be adding another little one to the family. She found part-time work with County Health taking care of an older gentleman, Rex, on weekends. He was legally blind so she would tend to his medical needs and make meals for him. It was a job that enabled her to take Mitchell along. Rex and Laurie developed a close friendship.

It was hard to believe that as August came and went, Mitchell was now four years old. After our annual community celebration of Fisherman's Picnic was over, things quieted down somewhat. With the added manpower on the department, one could actually get away for a few days. In November, we went to southern Minnesota and visited Laurie's sister, Chellie. I also ran over to Marshall for a quick duck hunt with Lee. Laurie was getting farther along in her pregnancy so we would spend the Christmas season at home this year. As 1979 drew closer, I was anxious for our new addition to the family.

9

MIXED BAG

In the early morning of January 19th, 1979, our second son was born. Richard Ernest came to be known as Richie. I still look back on the births of my two sons as some of the happiest periods in my life. After Richie was born, Laurie chose another way to make some extra money. In addition to her home health job, she started doing day care in our home. That was demanding but allowed her to be a stay-at-home mom. Mitchell was only four and a half, but he was a big help to her.

The Spring of 1979 brought some unusual incidents that kept those of us in the sheriff's department in a continual learning mode. I refer to a learning mode because we were all somewhat inexperienced yet. In April, the trailer of an 18-wheeler burned up on the highway three miles east of Grand Marais. A trucking firm hauled large rolls of paper from Canada into the United States via Highway 61. It was common to see these trucks. Sometimes a trucker would get tired and take a nap along the road in the cab of the truck.

On one such occasion, someone thought it clever to sneak into the trailer of one of these trucks and light the edge of a paper roll on fire. These rolls were huge and tightly packed so it wasn't as if they would explode into flames. In this case, the part of the roll that was lit, smoldered. The person who lit this roll left the rear door of the trailer open. When the trucker started driving, the breeze caused by the open door fanned the smoldering roll of paper and in a short distance, there was a raging blaze that engulfed the entire trailer. Fortunately, the driver saw the fire in his mirror and was able to stop and separate his tractor from the trailer and get that part of the rig safely away. How do you catch someone who does something like that? One way might be to offer a reward. I placed a call to the owner of the trucking company. I asked them to inquire with their insurance company if they would consider offering a reward for information leading to an arrest and conviction. The company put up a substantial reward and a few days later, I received information identifying a suspect. I met with this person and got a confession. We made an arrest and the reward was paid, no questions asked.

May provided action in the form of a plane crash. Thank goodness we don't see a lot of that kind of accident. No matter what reason we had for going into the woods, even if it wasn't very far in, it was always so difficult to get the equipment you needed to the site. This crash occurred just above the Grand Marais city limits near an area known as the old ski hill. The terrain near Grand Marais rises substantially as you leave the shore of Lake Superior. There is a mountain range called the Sawtooth Mountains that runs east and west through Cook County. The old ski hill was operated on the south sloping face of this mountain range. If the fog was heavy and dense sitting on top of these hills, a plane could fly into the side of the hill if the pilot wasn't aware of the sudden elevation change. I don't know if that's what happened on this occasion, but the plane went down before clearing the top of the hill. It was a small plane and there were three people on board. Two of them perished in the crash and one person survived but lost an arm.

The summer season came and always brought more people to this area. The population of the county increases considerably during this time of year and puts stress on all the emergency service providers. That is one reason we were thankful for the development of the Tofte rescue squad. The summer of 1979 also saw the arrival of the new Hovland Fire Hall. Little by little, we were improving services to people.

The sheriff's department continued to gather information regarding the thefts from vehicles parked in remote areas that had been going on since I moved back. A big break came in this investigation and arrests were made. This activity pretty much ended.

Back on the homefront, Laurie and I continued to enjoy our boys and each other. We found time for family to visit and time to get out of town for visits. It was so much fun to see Mitch and Richie together. I and some buddies took Mitch on an overnight fishing trip to a friend's cabin. We caught walleyes and made some good memories.

Little by little, we worked on our small house trying to fix things as we could. I discovered why, when you buy a house, you should look it over thoroughly. I hadn't looked into the attic of this house prior to buying it. During a March windstorm we awoke to a yard full of shingles. When I checked the attic, there was only two inches of paper insulation, and the heat was going through to the inside of the roof. This caused frozen condensation and the shingles came loose. I guess when fuel oil is only nineteen cents a gallon, you never worried about insulation. We had the roof repaired and added lots of insulation which made a big difference.

The Fall season of 1979 marked the third Halloween season I experienced since returning to Grand Marais. It was always fun for the little ones to dress up and go out filling up a bag with goodies. On West 7th Avenue, we had plenty of kids come to the door. As far as this time of year and my job went, I discovered another aspect of this season that had taken root. Gate Night. How and when this activity started in the community, I have no idea. I do know that what used to be kind of a mild prank night the evening before Halloween had become a period of very nasty, bordering on evil, behavior. Waxing windows and throwing crab apples had escalated into deeds bordering on felony behavior. Things like doing damage to vehicles, setting large tires on fire and rolling them down the streets of town and various other forms of property damage. There was a group of young people, not necessarily high schoolers, who seemed to resent a regular police presence in town and this seemed to be their way to act out against authority. It took a few years for this nonsense to calm down. Some of these troublemakers ended up getting caught and most of them finally grew up. For some it took longer than others.

When the winter of 1979 gave way to 1980, I would discover events that would change the way I looked at my job forever.

10

DARK DAYS

Since the BWCA legislation in 1978, The federal government began buying out businesses. These included End of the Trail Lodge, Kirk's Landing and Chik-Wauk Lodge. I remember thinking these were landmarks for so many years up the Gunflint Trail and kept hoping something would happen to change the way things were going. Then in March of 1980, McFarland Lodge located up the Arrowhead Trail sold out. In April, Hedstrom's Lumber laid off thirteen employees. It seemed as though with every business that was bought out, the fight went out of the locals to resist. On a positive note, the Gunflint Trail Rescue Squad was formed. Also, the U.S. Coast Guard was still maintaining a fulltime seven-man lifesaving station on the Grand Marais harbor.

Dark days were to follow. Our next-door neighbors to the south of us consisted of a couple and three children. Whatever difficulties they may have been dealing with weren't apparent. The husband appeared reserved but always ready to say hello and chat briefly. The kids were two boys of ten and a girl in her early teens. The mother was very pleasant. Laurie and I got to know her better than her husband. In previous conversations with her, I learned she and I had actually lived across the street from each other when I lived in International Falls. I was a few years younger and never knew her then. Our son, Mitch, who was almost six now, would play with these boys on occasion. One day the mother became concerned for her husband's welfare and asked if I would check an area where he liked to go. The sheriff and I went to a remote area of the county and located my neighbor parked on a rarely used road. He had ended his life by using carbon monoxide poisoning. That was very difficult for me to deal with. I always thought there was something I should have noticed. This offered me a look into the mindset of a person facing tough times. The wife and mother of this family was a brilliant woman and eventually managed to secure a very good job. Late spring and early summer were tough periods for the kids. I couldn't imagine the pain they were going through and words never seemed adequate.

When you work in a tourist area, holidays such as the Fourth of July bring increased activity. Throw something out of the ordinary into the mix and very busy can become hectic. Such was the case on July 6th, 1980. Our department never had enough manpower for 24-hour coverage so someone was always on call during the odd hours. When my phone rang shortly before 0530 am on July 6th, I felt something serious must have happened. Answering the phone, the dispatcher informed me that a shooting victim was at our local hospital. I responded to the hospital minutes later and went to the emergency room. I observed a doctor tending to the victim and another man was standing nearby. The shooting victim on the table was conscious but uncooperative. When the doctor was examining him and turned him on his side, I observed a wound on his back that indicated the bullet had gone through his body. This man had been shot twice, one wound in the chest and one in his lower torso. Given the severity of the wounds, I tried to take a dying declaration from him. He said, "Screw you, I don't talk to cops." I removed the other man to the hall outside the emergency room and asked him who he was and what happened. He identified himself as a local man from the Hovland area and told me he was the shooter. Hovland is a community eighteen miles east of Grand Marais. Since my return to Cook County in 1977, there were several people living in the county I had not met, and this fellow was one.

I was advised that the doctor was going to stabilize this patient as best he could and transfer him to a Duluth hospital. This is standard procedure for more serious cases as we have no surgeons at our facility. I took the admitted shooter to the law enforcement center for questioning. Prior to doing that, I called Floyd Bowman, a BCA agent in Duluth, and notified him of the situation. I requested he go to the hospital in Duluth and try to secure a dying declaration from our victim because he had refused to talk to me.

I read the shooter his constitutional rights as per the Miranda warning and he agreed to tell me what happened. He informed me that the man he shot was a friend of his who had traveled to Cook County to visit him over the 4th of July holiday weekend. A group of friends, including the man he shot, had partied at several locations. He told me this man had been drinking a lot and was known as a user of various types of drugs. After a couple days of continuous partying, this man became obnoxious and argumentative. The shooter, who was married, didn't want his pregnant wife and some of the other women in the group exposed to any more of this man's behavior, so he dropped the women off at another friend's house a few miles away. He returned to his house with the man he eventually shot and another friend who was also visiting. Early in the morning of the 6th, he and his friend convinced the drunk friend to go up into the loft and get some sleep. This home is a small place that has a landing as you enter. A person can either climb a small ladder to the left and go up into the sleeping loft or go to the right and walk down a few stairs into a small kitchen-living area.

As I'm speaking with this man, I'm observing he's a robust, active outdoors kind of man. He appears to be in his late 20s, perhaps early 30s and physically strong. He told me that he had easily been able to physically handle his intoxicated friend. He shared there were weapons in the loft where his friend went to sleep. That concerned him so he grabbed a semi-automatic .32 caliber pistol, loaded the magazine and put it in the gun. He kept this weapon nearby, then went to the bedroom below to rest and asked his other friend to keep an eye on the situation. He hadn't been down long when the guy in the loft was up and being obnoxious again. The shooter told me that he returned to the kitchen area. The fellow from the loft was now standing on the landing and wanted to continue partying. They argued and the guy on the landing picked up a heavy thermos that had been sitting there and threw it at him. He ducked, drew his weapon and shot the guy. The man fell from the landing onto the kitchen floor. The other friend who was sitting at a table next to the shooter witnessed this and said "You just shot your best friend! We need to get him to the hospital" to which the shooter replied, "No, let the fucker die."

At that point, the witness to the shooting got up and went out of the house. He was going to walk to the neighbor's house where the rest of their friends were staying. During a conversation I had later with this witness, he told me as he was walking down the driveway after leaving the house, he heard another shot. Meanwhile, inside the house, the victim was writhing on the floor, and the shooter had walked over to him and shot him in the chest area. He told me he then stayed with his friend and tried to talk him into dying. He said after some considerable time, he took him to the hospital where he then met me. Our conversation was a taped statement. I asked the man for permission to go to his residence and look at the scene and he gave me the okay to do so. I called the county attorney, filled him in and proceeded to the home where the shooting took place.

I and another officer spent a considerable amount of time doing the crime scene documentation. We took a lot of pictures and made the home off limits until we were through with what we needed to do. We also recovered the pistol and noticed an indentation in the kitchen carpet. This mark was consistent with what a projectile such as a bullet would make. I took a picture and cut that piece of flooring out. Later in the afternoon, when I returned to the office, I was informed by the sheriff that the shooting victim had died. The medical examiner confirmed that this man died as a result of the two gunshot wounds. He was still alive when he arrived at the Duluth hospital but died in surgery.

As I continued this investigation, I reflected on other homicides that had occurred in our county since I became a deputy. I recalled the New Year's Eve shooting that was investigated by a private investigator where I tagged along. After that, there was the death that occurred in March of 1970. I was away at BCA school and had no hand in that investigation. That had been a domestic fight, and the woman stabbed and killed her husband. She was acquitted after a trial. The other homicide was the shooting of a local state trooper in 1973 when I had just left to begin work in Marshall, Minnesota.

I was the lead investigator on this Hovland area shooting case. Of course, I had a lot of help along the way but the one thing that was always in the back of my mind was, "Don't screw it up!"

An investigation of this nature requires many tasks. Through this case, I met a man who was to become a mentor to me and a good friend. Floyd Bowman, a BCA agent out of Duluth, was an officer I first met when I was dispatching for the Grand Marais Police Department. At that time, he and his partner had been in the county investigating the deaths of two women who had perished in a motor vehicle accident. Floyd was not only a valuable resource for his knowledge base, but he was well known in the state and had many helpful contacts, including his access to the BCA crime lab. He was also respected by defense attorneys in the area.

The investigation involved tracking down many witnesses to corroborate stories, executing search warrants, taking pictures, having evidence examined and then double checking if there were obvious things that we missed. In between, there were court hearings, bail hearings and a new prosecutor to meet. Our county attorney came from the same area of the county as the shooter and was acquainted with him. To avoid a conflict, the case was handled by an assistant from the Attorney General's office. In addition, a grand jury was convened to determine the ultimate charge. That was scheduled for August 6.

Our investigation required several meetings with a defense attorney, question and answer sessions with the BCA agent, and various court appearances. Floyd introduced me to the defense attorney whom he knew. This man was a highly regarded lawyer from Duluth and, I must admit, treated me with respect. I liked him. Meanwhile, several other calls came in that required attention. When you work a case like this during the peak of a busy season, there is a lot of stress.

Busy became hectic. Just because one important investigation is going on, it doesn't mean everything else is going to stand still. On July 11th, the sheriff's department responded to a drowning a few miles west of Grand Marais. Several of the rivers that flow into Lake Superior have fairly significant waterfalls that drop into a pool and empty into Lake Superior a short distance later. These pools are tempting to swim in but are dangerous due to undercurrents caused by the waterfall. Our victim on this call was a local teen who had been drawn under by just such a current. Every one of these recoveries is different depending on the season and the amount of rushing water one has to deal with. Some of these pools can be examined by a diver if the water coming into the pool isn't too violent. At other times, officers try to retrieve the body out of the pool with a grappling hook. Due to the number of seasonal visitors to these rivers, we rarely have the luxury of time. This young man was recovered in a timely manner however. Every time a victim is local and, in this case, just a youngster, it hurts that much more. If, as they say, it takes a community to raise a child, the community also feels the pain when we lose one.

Hectic continued. On July 16, I received a call early in the morning to inform me of the death of a man and an injury to another who had been camping on an island on Saganaga Lake. Sag, as the locals refer to it, is a very large lake located at the end of the Gunflint Trail out of Grand Marais. It's a jumping off spot to the Boundary Waters and has many camping spots for boaters and canoeists. There were some violent thunderstorms moving through the area at this time and I was informed this man may have been killed by lightning. The survivor of this camp was taken to the ranger station in Quetico Park on the Canadian side of Sag Lake. Canadian authorities contacted U.S. Forestry personnel in Ely, Mn. and a forestry pilot flew this man to the Grand Marais harbor in a float plane. He was transported to the Grand Marais hospital. While this was going on, I proceeded to the lake with some trepidation as it was still stormy, and lightning was present. I went to Voyageur's Landing and spoke with Don Enzenauer, the business owner, who rented boats and campsites. He hooked me up with a boat and he and I went to the island to retrieve the victim of the alleged lightning strike. There was a stiff wind and a fairly rough patch of the big lake to travel over before we reached the island. I don't mind admitting my guts were in a knot every time a thunder blast went off and lightning flashed in the sky. I recall thinking, "What's the rush? This guy is dead and not going anywhere."

We reached the island, and it looked like it had been under attack from artillery. This was a duff covered rocky island and there were several areas that looked like the duff had exploded. Duff is a thick, mossy looking vegetation that grows over rocky terrain. If there are trees nearby, the roots will run under the duff. It would be easy to pitch a tent on top of a tree root and not be aware of the potential danger. In this case, that is exactly what happened. Lightning struck a tree, traveled down through the root system and exploded the duff where this unfortunate camper had laid his pillow. He was probably killed instantly. Later, when I had an opportunity to interview his partner, he said it was warm, so their sleeping bags were open a bit. The survivor had his hand across his friend's sleeping bag zipper and was awakened when the lightning hit. It traveled through the friend, down the zipper and entered the survivor with enough energy to temporarily cause lower body paralysis. He dragged himself from the tent and managed to crawl into his canoe. He paddled to a nearby campsite and alerted campers who summoned help. It seemed there was no end to the tragic events occurring this summer. I returned to Grand Marais with the victim of the lightning strike, thankful to get the heck off the lake. At times like these, I had to wonder why I left Marshall. Plenty of police work there but no wilderness adventures like this.

July rapidly ran into August and before I knew it, the grand jury hearing regarding our murder case was being heard. The grand Jury returned with an indictment of murder in the second degree. This was the same charge the state brought against the shooter originally, so nothing changed as far as charges went. Basically, second degree murder is the intentional killing of another person and does not require premeditation.

Between cleaning up some loose ends before this case went to a jury trial and resuming patrol duties, time flew by. Both of my young sons were growing up and August marked Mitch's sixth birthday. Richie was over a year and a half, and looking back, I realize how much time I missed with my kids and how much more of my wife's time they consumed. Thank God for her. She was the one who created so many special memories with the novelty birthday cakes she made and the great meals she always prepared. I didn't recognize it at the time, but she was my rock.

Continuing into August, the sheriff's office received a call reporting a vehicle stuck on a remote road in Grand Portage. A local resident spotted it and gave a license plate number to our dispatcher. When the plate was run, it came back to a vehicle wanted in a burglary of a sporting goods store in North Dakota. I went to the location and met a U.S. Border Patrol agent. We went into the woods, located the vehicle and observed a lot of outdoor sporting gear inside. There were two sets of human tracks on the soft logging road walking further into the woods. There was evidence of long guns in the car in the form of gun cases. We thought the two individuals could be armed and cautiously followed their tracks. As we came around a bend in the road, we spotted them about two hundred yards away heading back towards us. They were carrying long guns. We didn't know if they had rifles or shotguns, but the situation made the adrenalin flow. We quickly stepped into the woods and made a plan. We decided to let them get closer and who would shoot who if it came to that. When they were about thirty yards away, we stepped out. They were surprised and we took them into custody with no problem. As it is said, all's well that ends well.

The summer of 1980 continued to be busy. Stolen vehicles, burglaries and several drug-related arrests kept law enforcement busy. One of the burglaries that occurred in Grand Marais didn't amount to much as far as what was stolen, but it was the rare occasion when a fingerprint lifted from the scene resulted in an arrest. You see it on television all the time but in the real world, it's unusual. Jim Dalbec, one of the Grand Marais officers, had attended some specialized training regarding fingerprinting and lifting prints. In this case, he detected and lifted a fingerprint from a coin box in a vending machine and the case was solved because of that print. That is called putting a suspect at the scene with physical evidence. Good job, Jim.

In September, the sheriff's department received a call regarding an overdue employee. A young man working for the forestry out of Deer River had gone off on a Sunday evening and hadn't returned for work on the following Monday or Tuesday. We located the man's vehicle near a series of hiking trails by Oberg Mountain. This is a hiking area where there are several scenic vistas. It is 26 miles west of Grand Marais. The vehicle was located Tuesday night close to dark. We returned to search the area the following morning.

The vistas on the top of Oberg Mountain follow a circular path. This viewing area is on the summit of the Sawtooth Mountain Range as it parallels the shore of Lake Superior. On the face of these rock outcrops, pieces have broken away and littered the bottom of the cliffs over the years. The result of this erosion is a cliff with a sloped field of rocky debris around the base. We located this young man, dead, in a rocky area at the base of one of the highest vistas. It was extremely difficult to walk among the rocks as some were larger than appliances. We located a wash going down the side of the cliff and decided to take this victim up to the top and then go out on the trail which would provide much better walking. We placed the man in a body bag and managed to get him to the top of the vista. We then secured the bag to a stout pole and proceeded safari-like down the trail and towards our vehicle. The only thing that crossed us up was not putting anyone on the trail to prevent us from running into hikers coming our way. Sure, as heck, here came a group of hikers. To add more misery to this setting, our bag had torn during the haul up the cliff and partial exposure of our victim couldn't be avoided. The look on the hikers' faces said it all. It was one of those "you had to be there" moments. Based on the information we had available, this death was ruled an accident.

For an area that seems to have a day-to-day peaceful aura about it, the daily business of law enforcement begged to differ. Given all the activity of the year thus far, it seemed we weren't going to be able to catch a break. An example was a double fatality car accident that officers had to take care of in October. As preparation work was being completed for our July murder case due to begin in December, a major crime occurred in Grand Marais. A young woman was raped. The phone rang at 0630 am, which is never good when you're on call. This call was from Grand Marais officer, Jim Dalbec, who asked me to meet him at the local hospital. Although the crime took place in town, the suspect in this case lived out in the county. The deputies and local police always worked cases together when the situation called for it. This case involved a young working woman who was followed to her cabin in Grand Marais after she got off work in the evening.

Prior to following this woman home, the suspect who was a local man stole a rifle out of a vehicle that was parked downtown and used it during the commission of this crime. According to the victim, she was awakened by a man in her bedroom. This man was holding a knife to her cheek and demanded sex. The victim was assaulted over a period of three hours and threatened with harm if she reported it. When the suspect left the residence, the victim went to a friend's home and told her what happened. The friend told her they needed to report the crime. She took this young woman to the hospital and the police were notified.

Our victim knew her attacker and told us his name. Nevertheless, we showed her a photo lineup. She identified our suspect, and we went to the residence where he lived with his parents. The house was located several miles from Grand Marais and we were hoping to find him there. After arriving and knocking on the door, our suspect's mother answered and admitted us to the house. She woke her son who had been sleeping. We asked him if he would step outside and talk to us about an incident we were trying to clear up. Once outside, we arrested him.

This case began November 12 and resulted in more hearings, court appearances and trips up and down the road to Duluth. During this period, and even continuing to the present time, Cook County had no sitting judge. The nearest judge to us was in Two Harbors, 80 miles down the highway toward Duluth. Whenever an arrest was made and we had a time limit to get the perpetrator before a judge, we had to saddle up and head on down the highway. The only time we caught a break was when the judge came to Grand Marais on his regularly scheduled court days for our area. My recollection is that was every other Wednesday of the month.

1980 finished itself off with a continuation of sad, unfortunate events. In the first week of December, a young fellow died trying to save his neighbor's boat. This man was keeping an eye on things next door when he noticed a boat belonging to his neighbor had become loose and drifting in the lake. He lived along the shore of Lake Superior. On this particular night, a terrible December storm was raging and the wind was offshore. When this fellow noticed the boat starting to drift away, he ran over and jumped in the boat but discovered there were no oars or paddles in it. In moments, the offshore wind took him out into the lake and he had no way to get back to shore. The coast guard responded but had to stand down until the following morning due to the violent nature of the lake. The next day, the young man was discovered several miles out in the lake. He had died of exposure.

The December trial was quickly approaching and that meant the July murder case was finally going to be heard. Of course, I'm not privy to defense strategy so I don't know if it took from July to December for the defense to prepare their case or if they were waiting for the defendant's wife to have her baby, which she did, or if they were trying to get as close to Christmas as they could. Whatever, the trial began on December 9th and included introducing photos, statements, letting the jurors hear the taped confession, and testimony from witnesses, law enforcement, medical experts, etc. The trial lasted several days and went to the jury December 17th.

I recall at the time feeling confident about this jury. The case was well presented by the Attorney General's office and what I especially felt positive about was the jury getting to hear the taped statement when the suspect said "let the fucker die" with venom in his voice. A very short time after the jury got the case, we were advised they had a decision. Another good sign. When they came in with a "not guilty" verdict, I was absolutely stunned! I could not believe that this group of citizens was letting this shooter walk out of the courtroom. Were they confused because the victim died in surgery or were they just wanting to get on with their Christmas plans? I was interested in justice being done. I was just over eight years into my career, and I spent the next 18 years never trusting a jury again. That one took more than a couple of beers to ease the pain.

Toward the last day of December, the sheriff's department received a call from a concerned neighbor of a missing young man who lived several miles east of town. The neighbor went looking and discovered a leg sticking out of the snow. The sheriff and I responded to this site and retrieved the body of a 16-year-old boy. He died of a self-inflicted gunshot wound. There just seemed to be no good answers as to why some of these things happened. Suicides, drownings, murders, rapes, fatal car accidents, criminal sexual conduct cases, drug cases, and on and on and on. This was a far cry from my first year on the job in Cook County. What made this seem more tragic than my Marshall experiences was my personal knowledge of the people I was dealing with.

11

LIFE CONTINUES

I't's easier to remember some of the difficult cases because of the tragic circumstances, but there were other lighter moments that were taking place. Dolly Johnson, one of our beloved older dispatchers, was usually involved in community activity involving kids. I leaned in that direction myself and joined Dolly in some of her endeavors. In the 1980s, Grand Marais had a bowling alley and Dolly loved to bowl. She and some other adults started a junior bowler's program and had quite a few kids involved. Being in law enforcement, I wanted to interact with local kids and it wasn't long before I joined Dolly with the junior bowlers. In March of 1981, we took our junior bowlers to the State Junior Bowling tournament in Minneapolis. I don't remember if we won anything, but it was a great experience.

Another endeavor I undertook was chairing a St. Jude's Bike-a-thon for cancer research for children. I had received St. Jude's advertising in the mail and decided it was something I wanted to organize in our community. We ran our Bike-a-thon for three years in the spring of the year, usually the first weekend before Mother's Day. I had become friends with some young adults in the community who were part of "Young Life", a non-denominational Christian group. These young men and women were important to the success of the bicycle outings and were great volunteers.

When Laurie and I lived on the lower Croftville Road before we moved to Marshall, there was a family who rented some cabins next door. There was a boathouse on their lakeshore property and the owners let our group use it as a rest area during the bike-a-thons. The riders would get pledges and then ride to raise money. They would bike the Croftville loop, as we used to refer to it. This was a circular route of one and a half miles on the shoulder of Highway 61, then a turn onto the lower Croftville Road back to our starting point. The total loop was about three miles. After the ride, there was a recognition party in the church hall at St. John's Catholic Church. We had the support of several businesses in the county and they donated prizes for the top money raisers. All the bike riders got to participate in the 50-foot-long banana split my Young Life volunteers made. It was a good time and we usually raised close to $2000.

St. Jude's Bike-a-thon Raises $1,540

Peter Borson receives congratulations from Dick Dorr upon his winning the grand prize, a weekend for two at the Radisson Inn Grand Portage. Dorr, chairman of the St. Jude Bike-a-thon, presented awards and prizes to the 32 participants at a party on Thursday, May 8. Peter was able to make good use of the prize, giving it to his mother as a Mother's Day gift.

Mitch was going to be seven and Rich had just turned two as we headed into 1981. Though it was early in my career, I'm convinced it was the joy my family brought me that helped me along the way. With all the misery that kept rearing its ugly head, the love of my wife and kids brought things back into balance. I find these feelings more intense now when I look back on things after all these years.

We continued to make improvements to our two-bedroom home. Paint here, window curtains there, the kinds of things we could afford. There were never any trips to Disneyland on credit cards. Most of our trips were to central Minnesota to Laurie's family or to Wisconsin to visit my parents.

Laurie stayed busy of course with the boys and the day care service she was providing out of our home. When a person gets into that line of work, there is always so much to do. For the amount of effort she put into it, I don't think her income was ever close to adequate.

Things stayed busy for law enforcement going into the late winter months. The rape case investigation was ongoing, and I found myself running down leads on a burglary that took place out in Croftville. The theft, which occurred on December 28th of 1980, was of sterling silver dinnerware from a home. The fact there were fewer people in the area at this time of year and the identifiable property stolen gave me an edge and I tried to jump on it. A check of businesses in the Duluth area that deal in silver led me to The International Coin Shop. The business manager confirmed a man had recently sold them some silver. He described the merchandise he took in and made me think it may be from our theft. This shop was just getting ready to move the silver down to a smelter in Minneapolis, but the manager agreed to hold it for me. I brought the owners of the silver to Duluth and they positively identified it as theirs. I inquired of the coin shop manager where they conducted their banking business in the Duluth area and was directed to a bank in the Miller Hill Mall. I went to this bank and discovered our suspect had cashed the coin shop check there. This activity took place the day after the theft. A paper trail led me to the Shoreline Motel in Grand Marais where this man had stayed. I discovered this subject had a relative in our county in the Hovland area. I went to this residence and a search of this home produced our thief and an additional piece of silver that he kept. This case broke well for us. I arrested this fellow and locked him up thinking, "Every now and then, things go in your favor".

The arrest of our silver thief was on January 10th. In addition, our rape suspect of November 1980 pled guilty on January 28th and was sentenced to prison in Stillwater. God only knows there are many more intelligent folks than me working on the Minnesota sentencing guidelines, but this guy was sentenced to only 40 months. I could never get over how light a sentence people received for such vile sex crimes.

Even in the winter months it seemed as though there was always plenty going on. In just a few short years, it seemed the sheriff's department was making strides in hiring, bringing on two more deputies and trying to obtain equipment that would aid us in our job. An example of that was in late January, I and another deputy spent the better part of the day in Duluth pricing diving equipment. It sure seemed like the right thing to do as far as I was concerned, especially because of the water-related accidents we investigated.

Early February found me on the road again, this time to Stillwater State Prison with our convicted rapist. Whenever I had the occasion to make such a trip, I was always relieved when the delivery was made and I was out of there. There's something intimidating with hearing all those iron doors slamming behind you when you enter that type of prison. It puts freedom of movement in a whole new perspective.

Getting back into Cook County always felt good. A week later, I was enroute to Duluth again with a prisoner to be delivered to the Regional Corrections Center. The suspect from our silver theft pled guilty and I was off to jail with him. This seemed to be a pretty regular trip for all the deputies during this time period. Of course, the downside of all the road trips, aside from the expense, was that it meant an officer was away from the county for several hours. Most of the time we were always working a man short on a shift. When you were working the day shift, you had the sheriff to rely on as that was when he normally worked. If you were on the night shift, that meant you wouldn't have any backup if your partner was on the road. At the beginning of this particular year, I felt like a yo-yo as there were so many road trips. The latter part of February, I was sent to Duluth to participate in a skills management workshop. I returned home only to turn around and go on that junior bowling trip I told you about. It's no wonder a person became so familiar with the North Shore drive.

DEMONS PAY A VISIT

I can't put my finger on any particular reason, but I never liked the month of March. Looking at my career in retrospect, March of 1981 goes to the head of the class. To this day, I'm not certain I can identify why this month chose to be the entry period of a particular strife in my life but that's the way things fell. I was on patrol heading east one evening and all of a sudden, right out of nowhere, this feeling of dread came over me. It wasn't fear or panic but simply a feeling of dread that I couldn't explain. Was it because my head was still spinning from the period of the late 1970s and all the activity in the county? Was it based on the unbelievably difficult year of 1980? I have no idea, but I do know, all these years later, it is still a mystery to me. I've always been a person who likes to be in control of a situation and this new, unexplainable feeling took that away from me. I turned my squad car around and went home.

I figured I'd take off the rest of my shift and see if this crazy feeling would go away. It not only didn't go away, it manifested itself in a physical symptom. I became aware of an irregular heartbeat and the feelings of dread escalated into a death fixation. During quiet time, my heart would just hammer in my chest and I was certain I was going to die. I went to a local doctor and was assured I was in no immediate danger. Well, talk is cheap and there was no way I was convinced I was okay. I was given anti-anxiety medications and agreed to see a counselor. He advised me that perhaps I might pursue a new line of work, something less stressful. Right! Here I was, almost halfway to retirement, in a job with decent pay and good benefits and I should pursue something different? What would that be? What was available in Cook County at this time that I could do? It was probably good advice but, at the time, it just added to my stress.

The doctor recommended that I take some time off and try to relax. I was concerned that my boss was going to see this as a sign of weakness. Whether he did or not, when I gave him a doctor's order for needed time off, he granted it. I had been having conversations with the guys at work and they listened, but no one had any good answers. I felt guilty doing it, but I did end up taking a couple of weeks off and it helped somewhat. I worked through most of 1981 and '82 fighting these demons until I finally convinced myself I wasn't going to die.

DAILY DUTIES

The sheriff's department was still growing and we were trying to figure out how to operate efficiently. There became a routine for performing tasks that seemed to take us off the road for a lot of a shift. If there were prisoners, and there always were, the deputy on duty picked up their food, watched them when they took showers, let them out for visitor time periods and took them to various court hearings. If another deputy was tied up with a prisoner in court or performing bailiff duties, that left one deputy for patrol. If an officer was called away before he could get a prisoner's food, it would be delivered by the restaurant or one of the local town policemen would help us out. I recall thinking that these prisoners were being taken care of better than before they were locked up. Any little boo-boo and we had them up to see a doctor or dentist. Hell, we even let them out for smoke breaks. Probably the best thing about our prisoner contact was an opportunity to get to know them. If you treated them well, they remembered when they got out and it could make future dealings better. And, it seems, there were always future dealings.

Not all the time in the office doing these tasks was wasted. When prisoners were visiting or showering, we could take care of some of our tasks with phone calls. We also got to talk with and get to know our dispatchers better. We had a very dedicated dispatching staff. They were the messengers on the frontline when emergency calls came in. They worried about the officers when they sent us to a hot call or about local folks when accident calls came in. They also typed our reports which were no small task. In fact, it was a huge task. We generated a lot of paperwork in those days and they got to share all the good and the bad with us.

I can clearly recall one morning assisting the state patrol with a very bad accident in which a vehicle coming down a sideroad that entered Highway 61 in the Grand Portage area ran a stop sign and broadsided a vehicle with a man and his very young son. All were transported to the hospital. I went to the hospital to obtain blood samples from the driver who caused the collision. While checking on the father of the young boy, he asked me "How's my little guy doing"? It was not going well for his son and I don't recall exactly how I responded. The son had died. After I dictated this report and gave it to our dispatcher to type, I returned to the troop room. A short time later, I heard a sob coming from the front office and I suspected our dispatcher was going over the tough part of that report. It reminded me that officers weren't the only ones suffering on this job.

In July, I went on a call that I had a hard time believing. Toward the end of chapter 10, I mentioned a young man who committed suicide and the sheriff and I recovered him. During that investigation I canvassed the neighborhood where the victim lived in an attempt to see if a neighbor heard a shot to determine the time of the incident. This particular call took me to the home of the neighbor who had heard that shot. Now, ironically, he had committed suicide.

SURVIVAL SKILLS FOR HIGH SCHOOL SENIORS

Later in 1981, a 16-year-old girl and her two male companions from the Minneapolis area were kidnapped at gunpoint in the early morning hours when they were sleeping in their camper van. They had parked in an area in the village of Grand Portage. These young people were in the county to do some snowshoeing. Their vehicle was hijacked by a lone gunman and they were taken to a location along Highway 61. At some point, the two male companions and the vehicle were released. They called the sheriff's department and reported the crime. The gunman kept the young female victim and he took her to a cabin in the woods and sexually assaulted her during the early morning hours. Later that morning, the 16-year-old victim managed to escape and get to the U.S. Port of Entry. The sheriff's department was notified and arrested a local man for the abduction and rape. I thought about the rape that took place in Grand Marais just one year earlier. Both victims were young women who felt safe but ended up being victims. I wondered if there was information they could have had to be more aware. Also, what about all the young women who leave our community to go to larger cities to work or attend school? It seemed logical to me that they should be given some tools to increase their awareness and make them safer wherever they were going.

I had been working with the Cook County women's advocate on other issues and shared my idea with her. She thought it was a great idea and put together a grant proposal to the McKnight Foundation for funding. I contacted the school and asked if we could incorporate our "Survival Skills" program into the social science curriculum. Gary Peterson, the social studies teacher, was very receptive and we started putting our project together. Once the grant was approved, we contacted the University of Minnesota Duluth and made arrangements for personnel from that campus to address campus life issues such as roommates, safe study habits, homesickness and other college-related issues. We also had a female officer from the Duluth Police Department address personal safety issues and city smart topics like how to drive on a freeway, where to park and renters' rights issues if you lived off campus. It was quite a thorough program and involved two one-hour sessions per week for six weeks. We received great feedback and we were invited to do a presentation to the Minnesota Association of Women Police Officers at their annual convention. We also had regional media coverage through the Duluth television stations. Finally, something positive was coming off the heels of criminal activity. The program kicked off in the school year of 1982 and ran for three years until we just kind of ran out of gas.

An assortment of heavy duty locks is being demonstrated by Cook County Deputy Sheriff Dick Dorr in conjunction with an innovative program in urban living skills developed by Dorr county women's advocate Sharon Karas.

12
TOUGH TIMES

The term, "tough times" can have different meanings to people. We all experience periods in our lives dealing with difficult situations. My story isn't intended to portray my career in law enforcement as a "poor me" adventure. I'm trying, as objectively as I can, to tell you how this line of work can affect a person, particularly one who grew up in a small close-knit community.

According to the activities in the early 1980s, our deputies seemed to be playing catch-up in a county that never had much police presence. One way to gauge that was the chatter among some locals who were heard to say, "There are too damn many cops in the county." You could hear that on any given day. Aside from routine responsibilities of the job such as paper service, patrol duties, working traffic and the responsibilities of running the jail, we deputies handled a variety of complaints as citizens called them in. In addition, even though I was given the title of 'Chief Deputy' and sent to a specific crime scene processing school, all the officers performed investigative duties. It didn't take much to upset the apple cart as we never had adequate personnel, regardless of local opinion. From 1980 through 1984 there were 30 unnatural deaths which included 4 suicides, 2 murders, 10 drowning/hypothermia deaths, 3 falls, 6 motor vehicle accidents, 1 lightning strike, 2 carbon monoxide poisonings and 2 tree cutting related deaths. Some of these incidents could be resolved more quickly than others. Some deaths were going to require eventual courtroom resolution and needed an in-depth investigation. Any incident of this nature required a substantial report to help the families and the respective legal system achieve closure.

I always wondered what the next year was going to present. 1983 started out with a road trip to Lincoln, Nebraska to pick up a prisoner on an arrest warrant. It just so happened this trip took place on Super Bowl Sunday. It was a pretty uneventful trip, but it was an opportunity to see a different part of the country. February brought a domestic call, a crim-sex investigation, and a report of a stolen vehicle. Then, there was a blizzard in April! As the weather became more springlike, activity in the interior of the county picked up. Late in May, a teen drowned in Saganaga Lake. This was followed by two lost campers missing in the Brule Lake area. The first camper was found after fifteen hours on the first day. The second camper was found the next day. Both survived.

Searches in the remote areas of the forest usually involved personnel from Search & Rescue teams located throughout the county. State and federal foresters were also involved along with sheriff deputies. Often, we needed outside agencies to provide helicopters. Fixed wing aircraft was also used when available. Communication could be difficult when working in very remote areas. If there were any witnesses, we could use their information to determine a direction to begin a search and develop a grid pattern to work.

Prior to another anticipated busy summer season, Laurie and I made a quick trip to visit my parents in Chippewa Falls, Wisconsin. While there, I decided to check out a few clothing stores. In one department store, I was trying on a pair of dress slacks when I heard some commotion in the store. I peeked out of the dressing room and saw two police officers with two suspects in custody. One officer had a man handcuffed and the other officer was escorting the second suspect to the front of the store. I overheard a store clerk mention the word "shoplifters". It looked like things were under control so I went back into the changing room. Suddenly, there was increased noise in the store so I glanced out again. I observed the suspect at the front of the store break free from the officer and head back into the area where the other officer was. I was in a good location to assist so I jumped out of the changing room and tackled this subject. I held him down and the officer caught up with us and handcuffed this man. Both suspects were removed from the store. Quite the shopping story. Later, while still in the store, I heard a clerk ask a fellow worker "Did you see that activity in the store?" The worker pointed at me and said, "Not as close to it as 'that' guy." I had to smile to myself. After a brief visit, it was back to Grand Marais and what would amount to a very busy 1983.

City of Chippewa Falls

— 30 WEST CENTRAL STREET, CHIPPEWA FALLS, WISCONSIN 54729 —

July 1, 1983

Officer Richard Dorr
Cook County Sheriff's Office
Grand Marais, Minnesota 55604

Dear Officer Dorr:

I have been informed that on June 25, 1983, you assisted one of my officers who was attempting to place a suspect in custody at a local department store.

I want to express my personal appreciation and that of the entire department, for your willingness to get involved. It is good to know that the feeling of cooperation and brotherhood between law enforcement officers is alive and well.

Thanks again.

Sincerely,

Joseph S. Coughlin
Chief of Police

JSC:dk

I hesitate to say one incident is worse than another because when it involves death, it is still the ultimate loss. Words and actions never seemed enough. Three such incidents that stand out to me took place in 1983 within two and a half months of each other. They all involved young people and the decedents were all children of adults I knew in the community. First, came a fatal motor vehicle accident, then a drowning, and then a murder.

A motor vehicle accident in Grand Portage in mid-July was the start of a shift that would involve many hours of investigation. A young woman was seriously injured. She was 18 and died four days later. I questioned whether or not she was the driver. The seat of the car on the driver's side was pushed far back, an indicator to me she may not have been the driver. The owner of this vehicle was a large man which added to my suspicion. This case would involve meeting with the officer on duty that night and calling in an accident-reconstruction expert from the Minnesota State Patrol to assist with onsite investigation. Numerous witnesses were interviewed. The alleged driver of this vehicle was returning to a gathering after making a cigarette run. The deputy who responded on the night of the accident had blood drawn from the alleged driver and the results showed alcohol in her system. No one we interviewed stated anyone else at this gathering had been the driver. It seemed like suspecting and proving was going to be difficult in this case.

Four days after this accident, I was dispatched to Devil Track Lake to investigate a drowning. Devil Track Lake is a popular heavily used lake fairly close to Grand Marais. There are many homes and cabins on this lake and folks have fished, swam, and boated there for years. In late July, a young man had been windsurfing with friends. Witnesses said he fell off his board at one point and it drifted away from him before he could retrieve it. He fatigued and went down before anyone could get to him.

Those of us who knew the parents in both of these cases felt pressure to bring closure. If there was someone else driving the vehicle that killed the young woman from Grand Portage, we needed to do everything we could to find that out. As far as the drowning case was concerned, we wanted to recover the young victim as soon as possible and felt pressure to do that. These cases were going on just as the busiest time of the year, Fisherman's Picnic, was approaching. Fisherman's Picnic is a Thursday through Sunday event that occurs on the first weekend in August for former residents to return and reunite with the area and take in reunions with classmates and friends. In addition, there are hundreds, if not thousands, of tourists that participate in the event. I was thankful for the assistance of citizens and other officers in these cases, but you always felt ultimately responsible for the outcome. There were many long hours on the water and many trips back and forth to Grand Portage. I recall sensing the impatience of both families and who could blame them?

During the early morning of August 1, the body of our drowning victim was located by a friend of the family and was recovered. Recovery is certainly quicker if there are witnesses close to the location where a person is last seen. Obviously, a factor is also the water depth. Add other variables such as food content, lake currents and water temperature and some recoveries will take more time than others. I should note that Devil Track Lake is a fairly large body of water. If a victim of drowning surfaces, we still have to be able to locate him or her. Just about two years prior to this incident, a 14-year-old drowned in Devil Track and after several days of intense searching, he surfaced on a boat slip across the lake from where we located his boat. These types of cases are gut-wrenching because as you're working to resolve the situation, the families are suffering.

Most of August was spent on the Grand Portage accident investigation. The focus became centered on charging an individual at the outdoor party with supplying alcohol to a minor, specifically the young woman killed in the accident. In late August, our suspect was charged with giving and procuring liquor to a minor, one misdemeanor and one gross misdemeanor. In September, at an omnibus hearing, initial charges were dismissed stating insufficient evidence to support these specific charges. This left us with an opportunity to keep investigating, gather more evidence and recharge our suspect. I continued investigating. Several more witnesses were interviewed and new charges were brought against the subject. In May of 1984, the defendant pled to two misdemeanors.

This individual was sentenced to the Northeast Regional Corrections Center.

Regular patrol duties and new investigations soon presented themselves and I took some time off in September to take a breath and spend some time with my family. Even during these trying times, there were good things happening in my life. Earlier in 1983, Mitchell had made his First Communion in our church and Lee, my partner from Marshall, and his family came to Grand Marais for that.

We were also still in the process of putting our home together after a house fire in 1982. We had been out of town visiting Laurie's family and received a call from our neighbor that our house was partially burned and the damage was quite extensive. The fuel oil furnace had malfunctioned causing excessive fuel oil to spill out. The igniter finally sparked and started a slow burning fire. This furnace was in a crawl space under the kitchen and burned a hole in the floor. Oily discharge went through the house and our neighbor spotted the black smoke and called the fire department. The main structure was saved but the entire interior and our belongings were mostly destroyed. Black oil saturated everything. We moved into a vacant house across the street offered by a seasonal neighbor, jacked up our stripped-down rambler and made it into a split level home.

Mitch had a birthday on August 22nd and was now nine years old. Richie was four and our house was getting busier and busier. Laurie was back working part-time so work for me wasn't the only busy part of my life. Looking back, I wonder where a person got the energy to cope with everything.

Mitchell was entering the world of Little League baseball and I was the coach of his team, the Twins. Richie was not far behind and he kept us entertained with his dare devil stunts on our driveway with his "Big Wheel". Family time never seemed to last long enough.

More tragedy…

When the phone rang shortly after 2 am on September 30th, it was not good news. I was dispatched to the local hospital to investigate a shooting. It was a rainy night and I drove the few blocks to the hospital wondering what was awaiting me. As I entered the hospital near the emergency room, I observed some bedlam in the hallway. Several young people were standing around and were noticeably upset. From the period of time I had left the sheriff's department in 1972 until I returned in 1977, there were several groups of young adults I was still getting to know. This group, including the shooting victim, were in their 20s. I made my way into the emergency room and spoke briefly with the doctor. Our victim had been shot in the head and was being readied for transport to Duluth immediately. I went back into the hall, took one of the subjects, a young woman, into a quiet room and asked what happened. She identified herself as a witness and the girlfriend of the shooting victim. She told me an argument had taken place in the lounge downtown next to the liquor store. The argument involved her boyfriend and a guy she had dated in the past. There was some pushing and shoving and she and her boyfriend and two other male friends left the bar, got into her boyfriend's car and drove off. The next thing they knew they were being pursued by a vehicle that eventually ended up cornering them in a driveway off County Road 6. Her boyfriend got out of his car and approached this vehicle, a pick-up truck. All of a sudden, shots were fired, her boyfriend fell to the ground and the truck took off.

Information was coming in rapidly. What I learned from our dispatcher on the initial call was that the shooter had driven into town and turned himself in to a local officer on duty. So, I was aware he was in custody and I wasn't going to have to search for a suspect. What I was not aware of was that while I was interviewing this female witness, the other two men in the vehicle left the hospital and returned to the shooting scene to look for items of evidence that would later prove to be very important. They were also going to come up with a version of what happened that differed from the shooter's explanation.

Given the terrible weather conditions, I decided to go to the scene and record as much as I could. County Road 6 is a gravel road approximately two miles west on County Road 7 from Grand Marais and turns off to the right. This county road goes into the interior of the county and accesses County Road 8 a few miles up the hill. There are several driveways along County Road 6 that access homes. One of these driveways was the site of this shooting. While I located the driveway and examined the scene as best I could, the weather couldn't have been worse. Rain continued to pour down and my crime scene was being washed away. I located where the vehicles involved had been situated and where the victim had fallen after being shot. I took photos and some measurements and returned to the law enforcement center. There had been a deputy just going off duty when this shooting took place. When he became aware of what was going on, he met the city officer on duty at the law enforcement center and secured the weapon and other items of evidence from the shooter's vehicle. The deputy locked those items up and then signed off from his shift. When I arrived at the law enforcement center after examining the shooting scene, the city officer was there and told me how he had come in contact with the shooter. The citizen who lived up the driveway where this took place was coming home just after the shooting. They called in the suspicious activity and the city officer said he would check it out. Before he got out of the city limits, he met a pick-up truck that was flashing its lights trying to get his attention. The officer stopped and the driver of the truck, whom the officer knew, said he had just shot a man and he thought he had killed him.

This shooting victim did die, and the case became a homicide investigation. The ensuing investigation involved many hours and many interviews with witnesses. I called Floyd Bowman, my BCA agent contact in Duluth, and he provided assistance as only he could. There were very few rocks left unturned and no questions that were not asked. I recall we took a similar truck to the BCA lab in the cities and re-created the shooting.

The witnesses to the event gave inconsistent statements and when a Grand Jury convened, they perjured their testimony. It seemed as though everything that could go wrong did. The defendant even changed lawyers well into the proceedings.

Of course, a decision had to be made as to what charge would be brought. Was it first degree because the shooter initiated the pursuit? He went home, grabbed a loaded pistol, and chased down the victim. Or was it second degree murder, the intentional but not premeditated killing of an individual.

These cases are extremely difficult in one's small home-town community. Families on both sides have expectations of what they want, and any decision made was not going to go well with either side. As officers, we all had opinions, but the county attorney was the person who had to prove the case. I still had the bitter taste of the 1980 verdict in my mind and this case seemed way more mucked up than that one.

Something else to consider was the maximum or minimum amount of time one could serve. Even though back in 1983 second degree murder carried up to a 40-year sentence, a person could be released in nine years. That sentence is basically the same today. Nine years for killing someone intentionally hardly seems adequate. This came from the Minnesota sentencing guidelines structure that was introduced in 1980 for more uniform sentencing.

The eventual decision was second degree murder and eventually, the defendant pled guilty with no jury trial. The family of the victim was disappointed and the resulting political fallout of this case led to the election of a new county attorney. I understand the feelings of the victim's family and yet I was also aware of the incredible talent of this county attorney. The effects on cases like this linger for years. The mother of the shooting victim worked at a local grocery store and every time she saw me in the store, she started to tear up. I recall asking her if she wanted me to stop coming in and she smiled and graciously said "No, seeing you just always reminds me of what happened". Tough times indeed.

13

OPPORTUNITIES

As we got closer to the middle of the 1980s, the pace of our work didn't seem to lessen. The earlier part of 1984 was spent cleaning up the investigation regarding the 1983 murder. I probably keep repeating how frustrating it was to try and investigate an incident only to be drawn away by another. That happened with all of our officers. It didn't seem likely we would be establishing a permanent investigator position anytime soon.

Thinking of ways to promote safety in the community, I had an idea to introduce women with the workings of handguns. I thought it was important for them to know some basics so they would know what to do if they encountered a handgun. A participant didn't have to learn to shoot to participate. It was just as important to be able to identify different types of pistols and at least be able to know if they were loaded or not. Basic information in this class included the differences between a semi-automatic pistol and a revolver. It was a one-time class and just a few women showed up.

Sherri Pauling a student at Birch Grove school is being fingerprinted by Cook County Sheriff's deputy Dick Dorr. Over 500 students from the County participated in "operation childprint", conducted jointly by the schools and sheriff's department.

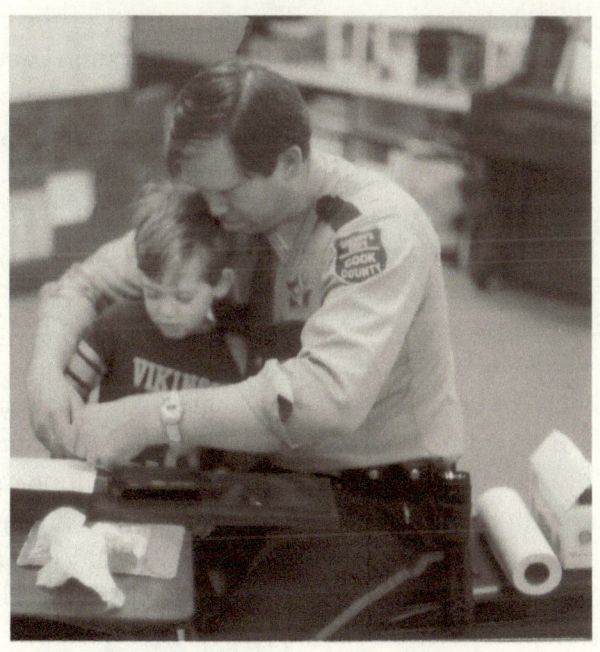

Another first-time program for Cook County was Operation Child Print. This was a voluntary project with the idea of being able to assist locating or identifying a child if they ran away, became lost or were abducted. Of the 530 children eligible, 333 participated. I considered it beneficial and a good opportunity to interact with youngsters.

Summers are always nuts in this county and some of our most common calls are responding to water accidents. In August there was a drowning in Cascade River and in September, a drowning in Brule Lake. In April the murder case concluded with the shooter pleading guilty to 2nd degree murder. The fatal car accident investigation in Grand Portage was also completed.

This became a year for me to travel. One trip took me to the state of Wyoming to pick up a prisoner. Earlier in the summer, a man from out of our county had spent time at a youth camp up the Gunflint Trail. He decided to leave and when he did, he stole a considerable amount of the camp's climbing gear. After interviewing those at the camp, I obtained information that he may be heading toward western states, specifically areas that were conducive to rock climbing.

This man's identification was sent to police agencies in western states, and we received a message from authorities in Jackson Hole, Wyoming that our thief had been identified in a park in their county. He was apprehended and held for us. My boss arranged a flight for me to go to the Wind River Range in Jackson Hole to pick up this prisoner. Little did I know I would be flying in a single engine Cessna. The plane was leased from a business in Duluth, Minnesota and flown by a pilot with military experience. In addition, he was familiar with the area we would be flying into. Flying over Minnesota at 4000 feet was comfortable. We landed in Rapid City, South Dakota to refuel. Flying over the Black Hills at 8000 feet into western Wyoming, however, was another story.

The Black Hills are not hills! When we got into the mountain passes of the Grand Tetons of Wyoming, we started to exceed elevations beyond 10,000 feet. Before taking off in Duluth, I made the mistake of reading too many charts posted on the walls. I recall reading that it wasn't advised to fly over 10,000 feet in a plane with no pressurization. I'm sure that pilot knew his limitations and felt very comfortable and in control. I was scared shitless! Flying through snow-covered mountain peaks made me wonder if my boss hated me. We flew into a stormfront before we reached Jackson Hole and had to put down in Dubois, Wyoming. There was a landing strip at the base of the Wind River Mountain Range and that was all. No buildings, no people, no telephones! Just as we reached the landing area, the wind hit and all hell broke loose! I thought "Just land this damn plane, don't do a flyover!" Well, he did a flyover and then attempted to land. The wind was so strong off the side of the mountain that the pilot had to quarter into it as we came down. When we were on the runway, he told me "When the plane stops, stand on the brake and I'll tie us down before we flip over." He managed to get that done and then the rain hit. We sat there for a brief period until the storm front passed and then thought about getting the word out that we were safe. My pilot was anxious to contact Air Traffic Control and give them our location. He said they didn't like it when a plane went off the screen suddenly. We walked about a mile down a switchback road before coming to a driveway that led to a local ranch. The driveway was long and in a remote location. We saw a house and walked up the driveway hoping to find a phone. I'm wired pretty tight by now and as we got closer to the house, my biggest concern appeared. There's never a long driveway without a dog at the other end. A German Shepard with a nasty disposition came running at us. I was dressed in street clothes but was packing (carrying a gun). I told the pilot, "Go for the house.

I'll shoot the dog!" Just then, a woman stepped out of the house and hollered "Dog!" I couldn't believe it! The dog came to a sudden stop. The woman invited us in to use the phone and my heart almost returned to a normal rhythm. The pilot made his call and our location was documented.

I contacted authorities in Jackson Hole to request they bring our prisoner to us by vehicle the following day. It was a very nerve-wracking experience for me. I am a nervous flyer and this type of adventure wasn't something I cared for. The next day, our prisoner was delivered, and I told him he'd better behave on the flight home or I'd throw him out of the plane! I made sure he believed me.

Later this year, another case took me east. A man employed by a business in the Blue Ridge Mountain area of Virginia stole a safe and tried to get into Canada through our county. He was stopped, detained, and subsequently arrested in possession of stolen property. The authorities from Virginia were notified and flew to Cook County to pick up their prisoner. Half in jest, I suggested if they wanted me to testify as to the chain of custody of the safe, they could subpoena me in the fall when it's beautiful out there. Much to my surprise, they did. I flew out of Duluth to Pittsburgh, PA and took a charter from Pittsburgh into Charlottesville, VA. My destination was a skiing and golfing resort called Wintergreen, a recreational area in the Blue Ridge Mountains several miles south of Charlottesville. When I arrived, I was given a key to one of their condos overlooking a large expanse of the forest and golf course. The Wintergreen Chief of Police provided me with a sporty car to drive. The resort gave me a credit card for meals, arranged a golf game for me and a tour of this historic area including Washington Lee University. I walked out on the balcony and listened to the sounds of the South in the live oak trees. It was magical to me. I hadn't been in this part of the country and at this moment, I wished my wife was with me. It was amazing!

The next day, I went to a small town to meet the prosecuting attorney. His first words to me were, "I appreciate right much y'all coming to our town." He went on to tell me the suspect in this case had entered a guilty plea and I didn't have to testify. No testimony from me was needed. He had an officer run to a café and bring us back an order of biscuits and gravy. The prosecutor showed me the courtroom. It was amazing! Its design and outstanding woodwork were straight out of the 1800s. The judge's bench was at least twelve feet high. There was a chair directly in front of the bench that witnesses sat in while being questioned. There were chairs on each side of the witness stand. I concluded this was where the term "cross examination" came from. This was an incredible experience.

In July of 1984, I had the opportunity to meet presidential candidate Walter Mondale. He decided to vacation at Gunflint Lodge approximately 40 miles up the Gunflint Trail. I was on duty when his plane landed at the Skyport Lodge airport by Devil Track Lake with his accompanying Secret Service attachment. The caravan that took him up the Gunflint was considerable. In fifteen minutes, the Secret Service agents installed a radio in my car that was compatible with their radio system. It was pretty impressive to see how they worked.

What had started to become routine activity in Cook County continued through the summers of 1984 and 1985. There were two bodies recovered at Two Island Lake and one at South Fowl Lake who succumbed to carbon monoxide poisoning due to improper ventilation. I worked a crim-sex case that involved an adult male taking advantage of a minor female. Her father brought this information to me after his daughter suffered emotionally and told him about it. The suspect was convicted of this crime. In June, a man drowned in Pine Mountain Lake and the sheriff's department recovered him on June 8th. The road into the lake was long and rough, making the recovery effort difficult.

On July 28th, 1985, a young man committed suicide in Grand Portage. I knew this man and worked with him. This caught me totally off guard.

A few days later, while I was parked on a street by the Holiday station in Grand Marais, I observed a young man get out of a vehicle that had Canadian license plates. He was dressed in a jean outfit, top and bottom. I noticed his pants appeared wet almost up to his knees. Being the son of a U.S. Border Patrol officer, I called a local agent and told him I thought this fellow may have just waded across the Pigeon River, the international border at Grand Portage. I followed this man until the local Border Patrol agent located me. I pointed the guy out and the agent approached him. It turned out this man was a Columbian National trying to go back home from Canada.

When I think of the many interactions deputies had with our Canadian neighbors, a couple of traffic stops I made come to mind. Both involved vehicles with Canadian license plates. It wasn't unusual to see Ontario plates heading down the North Shore to Duluth or continue on to Minneapolis. Deputies never set out to only work traffic as we didn't want to appear to be competing with the State Patrol. However, there was only one major highway going through the county and it provided the fastest way to get from one end of the county to the next. I had a personal philosophy. It was to stop only those exceeding the speed limit by a considerable margin. One very nice summer day shortly before noon, I was heading east on Highway 61 in the Croftville area. There is a considerable straight stretch on this section of the road and my radar unit picked up a vehicle I was meeting going 74 miles per hour. Seeing as that was 19 mph over the posted

55 speed limit, I hit the lights and turned on this car. The car pulled over and as I approached, I observed this car was from Ontario. It was occupied by a really nice-looking younger family, a man and a woman in the front and three youngsters in the back seat. I took the man's license to my squad and ran it to check his record. It came back clean and because he had been so cooperative on my initial contact, I really didn't want to write him a ticket. I approached the vehicle and looked into the back seat toward the children who were perhaps 6, 8, and 10 years old. I asked if they liked pizza. "Yes, yes, we love pizza!" was their reply. I told them that the money their dad saved by not getting a ticket meant he had to take them out for pizza that night. The parents gave me a big "thank you" smile and I was quite certain he kept his speed down the rest of the trip. I felt good after that stop.

All contacts aren't "feel good" however. On another summer afternoon I was patrolling east, almost in Hovland, when a car came around a corner very fast When the driver saw my squad, he locked up the brakes and blue smoke went up as he tried to slow down. I clocked his speed well into the 80s. This vehicle pulled over and it also had Ontario license plates. It was occupied by a male driver and a female passenger. The first thing this man did as I approached was flash a badge indicating he was law enforcement in Ontario. I listened to him briefly telling me where he and his girlfriend were heading. I asked him for his license, returned to my squad and wrote him a ticket for speeding. I walked back to his vehicle and looked across this man toward his young lady. I told him if I had a girlfriend that pretty, I wouldn't be driving like a maniac trying to kill her. I handed him his license and a ticket and left. He wasn't happy and I could have cared less.

1986 began with a duty that I didn't care for at all but at the time seemed necessary. We provided security at road crossings for the John Beargrease sled dog races. John Beargrease

119

is a historical figure from the North Shore area, a native Chippewa who delivered mail during a time when the only way of getting around in the northern terrain was by sled dog or snowshoe. The race was from Duluth to Grand Portage and back to Duluth. The mushers and their dog teams made strategically located stops along the way and negotiated several road crossings in our county. The race took place in January, the coldest time of the year. It wasn't unusual to sit in a squad car all night in 15 to 20 degrees below zero weather and help two or three teams cross a road. The first couple of times, it was a unique experience. After that, it lost its luster. Keep in mind, we didn't have iPhones to entertain ourselves. In the more remote crossings, we parked so we could see the musher's headlamp coming toward our location. As the dogs got closer, we would leave our vehicle and assist the musher's team with the trail crossing. There were usually just enough teams coming through to require staying alert. A music radio and a thermos of your favorite warm beverage were as exciting as it got.

When it came to the calls we received at the sheriff's department, I couldn't get over how different it was from when I first came on board in 1969. I'm not sure if it was due to the fact there were more people using our county or if our increased patrol presence discovered more activity. So many of the things happening involved fatalities of every nature. I just don't remember the numbers being like this in the past.

Late in January of 1986, I responded to a two-car accident on Highway 61 on a hill just before arriving in Hovland from the west. The accident involved a Canadian car and a vehicle driven by a local woman from Grand Portage. The woman from Grand Portage and one of the three young women in the Canadian car were killed. The Canadian driver pled guilty to criminal vehicular operation resulting in death. It always seemed surreal to me that a person you have been talking to just last week was now a fatality. These types of events really started weighing heavily on me.

Shortly after the above-mentioned fatal accident, I received a call that would require almost three years of investigating to complete. That story unfolds further in this chapter.

I responded to a fatal accident involving a local high school boy. It is a terrible feeling showing up at the door of a home early in the morning with a priest accompanying you. I think any officer will remember those calls as some of the most difficult.

Continued calls for assistance had the sheriff's department going out on a search and rescue for lost campers during a stormy day in July. While enroute, I was struck by a finger of lightning while gassing up at a local station. A major rainstorm was occurring and lightning struck near the canopy I was standing under. I think some supercharged water running off the canopy struck me in the back and caused my knees to buckle as I was entering my squad car. My hands were shaking and I told the Search & Rescue member with me, "I think I just got struck by lightning". He thought I was joking, but I said I was going to drive up to the hospital and get checked out. I felt strange. I had a mark on my back and some elevated enzymes. A brief stay at the hospital kept me "high and dry" the rest of that day. The lost campers were found safe.

1987 involved cases you will read about in my chapter of unusual cases. I did spend quite a bit of time on a case involving a local man we arrested for transporting drugs from Minneapolis to Cook County. After that case, I received a subpoena to go to Murray County, Minnesota, as a Spreigl witness. I still find it amazing how that case led to a similar outcome in an upcoming three-year criminal interfamilial sexual misconduct investigation.

One of the most difficult and important decisions a trial judge can make is whether to exclude or admit "Spreigl

Evidence" against a defendant. In a nutshell, this type of evidence has to do with introducing a defendant's previous bad acts. Does "Joe Blow" always settle his disputes by punching someone or worse? If "Joe Blow" has a history of that and he becomes involved in a serious situation because of that behavior, can some of his former victims be subpoenaed to testify to his past bad behavior?

My first encounter with Spreigl was in 1987, more than ten years after I left Marshall to return to Cook County. Back in the eighties some of you may recall a newspaper story of a young woman who made herself famous by sitting on a copier at work and taking a picture of her derriere. Someone in the media accessed this picture and made this young lady a temporary celebrity. At some point in her life, she ended up in a southern Minnesota town and was fatally shot. The shooter was a young man I had dealt with when I was a deputy sheriff in Lyon County. I was subpoenaed as a Spreigl witness to testify that this young man had violent tendencies. The case was a homicide and he was convicted, in part, because of the Spreigl evidence introduced against him.

Little did I know that a phone call from a young woman in 1986 would initiate an investigation that would introduce me to the devastation and despair an interfamilial criminal sex case could bring and the role Spriegel would play. The young woman called the sheriff's department one night and explained a concern she had. She was one of seven daughters born to a man who was now living in a remote area in our county. She told me that her father and mother were divorced. Her father, a retired teacher, married one of his students and moved to Cook County. She told me that prior to moving to Cook County, her father and his young bride lived in another area of the state. While they lived there, they had a daughter. She told me that one of her six sisters was visiting her father and observed inappropriate sexual touching of the baby by her father during that visit. She was concerned for the welfare of this child. Another part of her statement that got my attention was when she shared that her father had abused her and the rest of her sisters from the first marriage.

As all the girls were getting older, they started sharing that information with each other and some ended up in therapy. The information these women shared included being the victim of a multitude of sexual acts. These women were at a stage in their life where they were willing to speak with someone about these experiences. I informed her that I knew someone who could help with this matter and I would be back in touch with her soon. I had met several outstanding officers over the years and one such officer was a female investigator named Joelle Kohout, an agent with the Bureau of Criminal Apprehension. I felt this was a case she could assist me with. She certainly had more resources available than I did. These seven women were living in several states and taking statements would be no small task. I contacted Joelle and she offered her assistance. I put her in touch with the young woman who originally called and the process began.

Toward the end of 1987 and early 1988, Laurie and I started thinking about taking a family vacation. We had never done so and the boys were 9 and 14. We had worked a number of stressful years and needed to take a break. We arranged a train trip to Arizona where a classmate of mine lived. He and his wife were going to give us a two-week tour of the area. Even though I had some significant cases pending, we departed on our trip Easter Sunday, the second week in April 1988. That trip could be a book on its own so I included highlights in Chapter 21, Reflections.

Returning from our 1988 vacation to Arizona, I was curious about the results of an investigative tool I used pertaining to a suspect in a potential perjury case. The tool is called a "Mail Cover" and is an investigative aid the U.S. Postal Service provides to assist in cases that qualify for its application. It allows an investigative agency to watch a suspect's mail for a period of time up to a month. My particular case involved a person testifying in court about a lack of funds regarding the ability to satisfy a family matter. The mail cover showed me this subject received mail from a brokerage firm in a large city. I obtained a search warrant, went to that large city and executed this warrant. I discovered this person had a substantial amount of assets. This information proved my case.

Regarding the above-mentioned criminal sexual conduct case I received in 1986, I had interviewed the suspect to begin the process at my end. He was a former teacher and was very arrogant. At times like this, I enjoyed playing the not so bright small-town cop. I wanted to lock him into a story and see how things developed. It took a fair amount of time for the daughters' statements to be gathered. Meanwhile, I took another statement from this subject in 1988. I also interviewed his wife. When the statements from the daughters were completed, the State of Minnesota applied for and was granted an order to remove this suspect's young daughter from the home. She was examined by experts in the Minneapolis-St. Paul area. I don't recall the specific results but there was sufficient evidence to go forward with prosecution.

In 1989, the preparation for this case was close to completion. The seven daughters were going to be introduced as Spreigl witnesses. All of the daughters testified during the Spreigl part of the case as to what happened to them. I was in a room with them before and after they testified. It was some of the most intense emotional moments I've ever seen. I wish there would have been a way to record them as a learning tool for health care professionals and officers. It showed me what the abuse of a trusted family member can do. This made me think back to 1977 and the young boys abused in that youth camp. What were their lives like? They never had a chance to be heard.

This father was convicted of criminal sexual conduct and prior to sentencing, his attorney asked the judge if his client could go home and put his affairs in order before reporting to prison. He was granted permission and he went home and killed himself. The final act of a coward. I suppose it sounds jaded on my part but that was not a difficult body retrieval for me. This man was involved in some disgusting activity. There was no way for me to know, but I imagine this was a difficult conclusion for these young women.

14

UNUSUAL CASES

It isn't surprising to receive a call to investigate suspicious driving. It is unusual, however, when the erratic driving complaint is a vehicle being driven around in a pasture. That is what I discovered when I responded to a call one afternoon. A few miles west of Grand Marais, a man was off a county road and doing some off-road driving in his sedan. Fortunately, he became hung up on a log and I didn't have to drive after him. I parked along the county road and walked into the pasture approaching the stuck vehicle. The engine was racing and the man was trying to dislodge his vehicle. He was not able to do so, and I got him out of the car and turned the engine off. He appeared extremely intoxicated and was very unsteady on his feet. I was finding it difficult to understand why there was no noticeable odor of some type of alcoholic beverage. That mystery cleared itself up when I looked into the vehicle and noticed several empty bottles of mouthwash on the back seat. This individual had the cleanest smelling breath of any drunk driver I ever arrested. No wonder a person loses their breath if one swallows some mouthwash when gargling. When I examined the contents of these bottles, they indicated a 27% alcohol content.

This was a sad case when I considered how desperate a person becomes chasing that alcohol high. I know when I was smoking heavily, I never wanted to run low on cigarettes late into the evening. I needed to have one available first thing in the morning when I woke up. I suspect dependency is similar. I recall a conversation with one old timer years ago in his logging shack. I smelled a strange odor when he spoke. He had been drinking strained sterno (fuel for his cook stove) through slices of bread and drank what came through. Talk about alcohol poisoning!

Some interactions with citizens border on being spectacular and the following is an example. Regrettably, I didn't get this hero's name. On an August afternoon in 1983, I was patrolling on a road in the Maple Hill area a few miles north of Grand Marais. Several residents live along this particular road. While I was passing by a driveway, a man waved for me to stop. I pulled into his driveway and he told me that his mother, who was dealing with memory issues, had walked away from this house and he was concerned she may have wandered off into the forest. The area around this home was heavily wooded and as I was thinking of what to do, a vehicle drove by and stopped. I asked the man driving if he had seen a woman walking along the road and he said he hadn't. He asked what was going on and I told him a disoriented lady might be lost in the woods. He told me he had a hunting dog in the car with a pretty good nose and offered to see if the dog could pick up a scent. We retrieved a piece of this woman's clothing from the house, gave the dog a chance to sniff it and he took off into the woods. The dog located this lady in the woods after only minutes. Thanks to this man and his dog. You can call it luck, but I'll call it an act of God.

Another unusual case was Christmas 1986. I was called to investigate the Maple Hill church fire. This is a location in a maple tree growth about three miles north of Grand Marais just off the Gunflint Trail. This church is the heart of a large cemetery and is near and dear to many folks in the county. I could not believe that it had burned. Countless times on patrol over the years I would swing through this area because it was so peaceful. The hills close to the church and neighboring cemetery offer beautiful views. In the fall, I would often pull in and pick a few berries near an old homestead above the church site and just enjoy the beauty. There was evidence of arson at the scene in the form of several partially burned stick matches near the foundation and fresh footprints leading away from the church. I was able to follow the tracks to a house on Maple Hill and question the occupants. Two juveniles ended up being held responsible for the church fire. However, that discovery didn't bring much joy to anyone. This fire resulted in a lost treasure to the community even though a beautiful little church was built to replace it.

Some cases not considered unusual in certain jurisdictions are, by their nature, unusual in our county because they occur infrequently. One such case took place in Grand Portage. A seasonal worker was the victim of a home invasion, a strong-arm robbery. A woman came to the victim's door asking for directions. The victim told her he couldn't help her as he had not lived in the area long and was not familiar with many of the local residents. She left, and he returned to eating his supper when about 45 minutes later, he heard another knock at the door. When he opened the door this time, a man who appeared to be in his early twenties, stepped from the shadows, pointed a shotgun at him and told him to "make no funny moves". The man ordered him back into the house, accompanied by the woman who had earlier asked him for directions. The couple asked him for money and the victim directed them to the bedroom where the woman removed cash from his checkbook while her companion held the gun on him. After ripping the telephone out, the duo forced him to lay on the couch where he was bound and gagged.

Shortly after this, the victim was struck on the head with an axe and feigned unconsciousness until the couple left the house. He was able to free himself and called the sheriff's office from a neighbor's home a short time later. On the way to the neighbors, he noticed that his pickup truck was missing from the driveway and provided the sheriff's office with a description of the vehicle.

I called the U.S. Port of Entry with a description of the vehicle and set up a roadblock on southbound Highway 61 in case they should head that way. Before we had a chance to organize a roadblock on our end of the county, we received a call that the Canadian authorities did stop this vehicle as it attempted entry into Canada. The suspects were turned over to us and this case had a quick ending. Over the years, many people found themselves at a dead-end when they hit our international border. Lucky for us!

A case that would be considered unusual by any department's standard occurred in the summer of 1987. A young couple entered the BWCA wilderness area. The wilderness area is in the Superior National Forest and is approximately one million acres in size. Their entry point was Ely, Minnesota and they worked their way east to Saganaga Lake. "Sag", as locals refer to it, is in Cook County, fifty miles northwest of Grand Marais. This lake is very large and is popular in summer months with boaters and canoeists. Prior to the lake being incorporated into the BWCA, there were several large lodges and a lot of boat activity. Now, campers were seeking a wilderness experience and permits were necessary to access the area. During August of 1987, I was dispatched to this lake and proceeded to a particular island to retrieve a body.

Members of the Department of Natural Resources and the Gunflint Trail rescue squad also responded. This young couple decided to partake in a spiritual fast during their stay on this island. The couple, a man and woman, had been in the 13th day of this fast when the woman collapsed and the man summoned help from other campers on the lake. He was in a weak condition and was taken to the Cook County Hospital. The woman was deceased and we retrieved her body from the island campsite. I can still recall picking her up and how incredibly light she felt. There was nothing to her.

As I investigated this incident it was hard for me to understand how two intelligent young people had allowed this to happen. I interviewed the man in the hospital and discovered they had been in the woods since early June. They were spending the summer getting to know each other in the beauty of the wilderness. At some point in August, they decided to partake in a fast lasting 14 days. It was something they had read in the bible. The unusual thing was that the fast included no water which is unheard of. Particularly unfortunate was the fact that the woman collapsed on the thirteenth day of the fourteen-day fast. Doctors that she was in good physical condition as far as no food goes but severe dehydration causes cardiac arrhythmias and that is what she died from. Her friends indicated she was very knowledgeable as far as nutrition and taking care of her body. They said they could see her taking on a challenge like this and not giving up on it. Some friends of this woman were less accepting of this explanation of fasting and didn't think it sounded like something she would do. At the campsite was a log this woman was keeping of the fasting period. Each day, entries indicated how they were doing. In the latter stages of the fast, the entries became shorter and made less sense. I felt you could tell the negative impact that was taking place on her ability to think clearly. No charges were filed as it boiled down to a bad decision that became worse. I couldn't help but think of all the people that come to this area with great times in mind but end up in body bags. Now, I'm supposed to go home and have supper and coach Little League. What a job!

Another case that falls into the unusual category also took place in Grand Portage and was a suicide. This case involved a discovery made by personnel employed by the Grand Portage Lodge. A man rented a room and was not seen for some time after checking in. A check of his room led to an employee discovering him deceased. I responded to the lodge and observed this man in a bed hooked up to what appeared to be an IV (intravenous) setup similar to what one would see in a hospital. I did not know it at the time, but this man was a highly trained, very highly regarded flight medic for North/Hennepin County Medical Center. He was the chief flight paramedic for Wings of Care, a fixed wing ambulance service in the metro area. Some background information on this man indicated he was going through some tough times in his personal life. The fact that Christmas was right around the corner may have added to his decision. He used his medical skills to hook up an IV and infused medications to end his life. Several months after his death, a good friend of his brought the man's son to the area. He was looking for some closure and I tried to provide some. There never seems to be adequate words to explain suicide. It was humbling to think that this man's friend trusted me enough to try and help this boy.

A most unusual case occurred on October 28, 1995. Three guests, using a solo and a double canoe, went paddling on Gunflint Lake. These paddlers had reservations for a gourmet dinner at Gunflint Lodge and failed to appear at the appointed time. The assistant manager was informed by other members of their party and he immediately made arrangements for their

Gunflint guide to search for these missing canoeists. No one knew where they had gone. The guide searched vainly as it was getting dark. The lake borders Canada and he decided to take a quick look along the Canadian side. Just as he was about to return, he spotted two figures on shore waving frantically pointing out on the lake. The guide went closer and could finally see something bobbing in the water. He realized it was a person and approached with his boat. With great difficulty he was able to pull the semiconscious person into his boat. He hollered at those on shore that he would be back and took off for Gunflint Lodge. Somehow the two canoes had tipped over, all had life jackets, two had been able to get to shore, but the third person could not. It was estimated the female victim had been in the water for at least an hour and a half. There were some EMTs (Emergency Medical Technicians) in the Gunflint dining room enjoying their first course of their meal when the guide got back. They went to help. The patient had a very slow pulse. The owner of the lodge, also an EMT, ran for the ambulance. The patient was loaded in the ambulance that took off for the hospital 45 miles south to Grand Marais. The EMTs gave oxygen, monitored the vital signs and gradually tried to warm the patient. Halfway down the Trail, the patient went into cardiac arrest. CPR was initiated and continued all the way to town. Life Link helicopter was radioed to be sent from Duluth and for Grand Marais EMTs to meet the ambulance at the hospital to relieve the three EMTs who had been performing CPR during the trip down. Upon arrival at the hospital, appropriate medications were given in the ER and CPR was continued. The patient's body temperature was so low that it did not register on the hospital's hypothermia thermometer. The Life Link helicopter paramedics continued CPR all the way to Duluth. The ER personnel were able to treat the patient so that two weeks later she left the hospital with no ill effects from her experience. Cook County is indeed fortunate to have the many dedicated EMS personnel in the community and at the hospital who respond at all hours of the day and night to help their neighbors and visitors.

15

BUSTED

Throughout the 1980s it was illegal to use or possess marijuana. Living and working in a community with an international border crossing, drugs showed up in many ways. Through the air, on the water of Lake Superior or on Highway 61. Often authorities came in contact with illegal drugs when someone was either crossing the U.S. border into Canada or coming into the U.S. from Canada. If these people and their vehicles were searched and any drugs, such as marijuana were found, they were charged with possession and in many cases their vehicle was seized. This type of arrest was quite frequent and became known as a "border bust". Our deputies made many trips to the border when U.S. Customs and Immigration officers made a seizure of this kind.

In addition, there were a number of people in the county growing their own marijuana. Who knows how many of them were never detected. It wasn't unusual to find "pot" growing in remote locations. Every now and then, something substantial would come along such as the hash oil discovery we made in Grand Portage.

As far as the Canadian drug trade went, the process was usually the money came down to the States and the drugs went into Canada. A case that stands out is one involving a large quantity of hash oil. To use this marijuana derivative, a person would drop a line of the black, tarry drug onto the paper of a cigarette. It would absorb through the paper and into the tobacco and be smoked. It was quite popular for a time in the 80s. One day, the sheriff's department received a call from the Grand Portage Lodge regarding a discovery made by an employee. A housekeeper was cleaning a room thought to be empty. In the process of doing so, the employee discovered a package under a bed. A manager was summoned and the package was partially opened. The contents were suspicious to him and upon further checking, he discovered the room had been rented to a party from Thunder Bay, Ontario. The sheriff and I responded to the location and examined the package in the room. It appeared to be hash oil and we tested it. We had a positive test result and discussed the best way to proceed with this developing situation. Should we arrange to watch and document who picks up the package and then have Canadian authorities follow the dope to a destination in Canada or should we sit on it and apprehend whoever comes to pick it up? The problem was we had no idea how much time we had to work with before someone showed up.

Due to the uncertainty involved, we decided to sit on the dope and work the case up as it played out. I stationed myself in a room directly across the hall from the room containing the drugs. The sheriff left to make calls to other authorities and positioned himself at the border. Soon another deputy joined me and we began our wait. After a few hours, a couple showed up, ate supper at the lodge and went up to this room. They picked up the package and as they attempted to leave with the package, we arrested them. We learned that a man in Thunder Bay, Ontario brought the hash oil with him from Florida as far as the Grand Portage Lodge. He rented a room and proceeded to his home in Canada. He then sent some friends to the lodge to have dinner on him and asked them to pick up a package for him. We learned the man's identity, eventually had him extradited to the U.S. where he was tried and convicted. I don't recall the penalty he received. The hash oil weighed 18 pounds and at that time and possibly to this day was the largest seizure of its kind in state history. All this happened due to an alert employee. You can bet that is just a tiny fraction of the drugs smuggled through our county and across the border.

There are cases to be made by being in the right place at the right time. One lovely evening in October 1989, I was parked in a field approach along County Road 6. There was a driveway into a residence not far from where I was parked. The driveway into this home was long enough so the house couldn't be seen from the road. It was quite late, and I wasn't planning on anything in particular before ending my shift. To my surprise, a vehicle came from this home and turned onto the county road and passed in front of me. As a normal reaction, I took down the license plate number as this vehicle drove by. I was curious who was coming out of this location so late. The name the dispatcher gave me identified the vehicle owner as a person I knew who had been involved with drugs in the past. This made me curious as to who lived in this home. The next day, I went to the courthouse and identified the owner of the home. I discovered this individual was out of the area taking care of personal business. The following evening, I drove into this driveway to check the status of the house. I parked near the front of the house and observed a padlock on the exterior entry door. Everything seemed in place as I looked around this building.

Examining this property further, I noticed a large two-story detached garage. This building was located several yards away from the house. Under the roof, at the peak of the garage where there could have been a window, the opening was boarded up and an exhaust stack protruded. I approached this building and as luck would have it, the two garage doors had glass windows in them so I could see into this building. I saw a stairway going to the upper level and a very substantial padlock securing that entry point. This was getting more interesting. I walked around to the back of the building and discovered an older, longer ladder lying at its base. I observed a similar vent coming out of the rear peak area. Knowing the identity of the fellow I saw coming out of here, I started thinking this may be a marijuana drying site. I put the ladder up and climbed a few feet when a whirring sound suddenly occurred from inside. It sounded similar to the whir of an electric motor. It was late in October so this would be a good time of the year for a marijuana drying operation. I felt I had probable cause for a search warrant. The next day I prepared a probable cause report and obtained a search warrant. I watched this site on my next shift thinking my suspect might return. He didn't and I and several officers executed the warrant. When we snipped the lock on the door leading to the upstairs, a very strong odor of marijuana came from the opening. We discovered a relatively sophisticated hydroponic marijuana growing operation. The entire interior of the upstairs had reflectorized material on the walls along with grow lights and nutrient-supplying hoses on timers. There were several large barrels of water under the stairway that fed the plants. There was a large garbage container near the plants that had packaging material addressed to the person I saw leaving this area a few nights earlier. This package came from a headshop in Seattle, Washington and gave us probable cause for another search warrant for that home in Grand

Marais. We videotaped our search and removed several dozen mature plants from this location. I returned to the office and applied for another search warrant for the residence addressed on the box at our original search site. Before executing that warrant, I contacted the U.S. Border Patrol in Duluth and requested the use of their drug dog. We executed that warrant and discovered marijuana bagged up in the basement in a filing cabinet. We had the benefit of keeping an eye on folks that we were told may be involved in drug activity. One of our frustrations, however, was knowing and proving it. This was one time we could prove our suspicions.

A very short time later this same month, Cook County deputies assisted a multitude of federal agencies in arresting a man who was operating a money laundering/drug operation through his commercial fishing business. This man was operating on Lake Superior out of Grand Portage. He was alleged to have transported large amounts of marijuana and cocaine from Florida to Northeastern Minnesota in the 1980s. We assisted agents of the IRS, BCA, and DEA along with the Lake County Sheriff's Department in seizing items from his charter boat business, his home and vehicles in Lake County, along with $40,000 in cash. This case was interesting because it showed the kind of activity that had been going on in our area throughout the 1980s. We would frequently receive information from citizens concerning suspicious lake and air activity but seldom had the resources to respond. It was very important for our department to develop contacts with these state and federal agencies. They had more ability to act on good information. This man was convicted in federal court and sentenced to seven years in the Duluth Federal Prison Camp. He admitted his involvement in an eight and one-half year drug conspiracy and to laundering $85,000 in drug proceeds in 1987.

In the front of my book, you can see a list of the agencies I called on for assistance during my career. Most, if not all of them, were much larger than my department and had unique capabilities specific to their agency. As I mentioned earlier, the regional postal inspector could assist with mail covers if the investigation warranted one. If someone appeared to be living way above their means, I would call an agency that dealt with financial matters and suggest putting this person under a microscope. I received calls from investigators informing me of people in our county who had made phone calls to subjects involved in organized criminal activity. It didn't surprise me. When you work in a major destination area with only one highway that connects your community to another country, the bad element is coming over the same road as the innocent visitor. Criminals think remote counties like ours are good places to do business.

16

MY 20ᵀᴴ YEAR

As the 20th year of my career approached, it was impossible to even try to guess what might be in the future. Looking back on that time I was about to discover that things could always get worse. After a couple of important cases concluded with court activity, I took a week off in November of 1989 for deer hunting. Sitting in my deer stand watching the season change was therapeutic for me. Spending hours in the woods gave me time to reflect on life as it was playing out. November 19th was my dad's birthday and after a successful hunt, I was looking forward to calling him. However, my dad called me first to inform me Mom had suffered a major brain bleed, was in the hospital and the prognosis wasn't good. Stunned, Laurie and I took off for Wisconsin the next day. We arrived in Chippewa Falls and went to the hospital. Mom was in a coma and we had to help make the decision to turn off the life support machines. That was very difficult and we watched Mom pass one hour later. She was 72. The fact that this had occurred on Dad's birthday made everything seem surreal. Dad had just turned 68 and was dealing with major health issues of his own including arthritis and heart disease. Prior to Mom being struck down, Dad had been in and out of the hospital. I wasn't sure what to do. We stayed a few days after Mom's passing and planned on returning at Christmas. Dad ended up in the hospital just days before our Christmas visit and we concluded, in addition to his own health issues, he wasn't dealing with my mother's death very well. However, we had to return home due to the boys attending school and our jobs. Dad got out of the hospital shortly after we returned home. Some of his good friends were keeping an eye on him for us while Laurie and I decided if we should have him move in with us. On March 21st, I received a call from the hospital saying my dad had been admitted once again. I thought I'd wait until later in the day to see how he was doing. An hour or so after the initial call, the attending physician called to inform me Dad had passed away. That took my breath away!

My lifelong hero was gone and I was devastated. First, my mom, that hard working German woman who always made our home special. She was a devout Christian who always put family first. Now my dad, the guy I knew who was never going to die. He bought me my first baseball glove, took me hunting and fishing and came to all my athletic games. I had a private session with him in the mortuary before his funeral. I slipped my graduation picture into the inside pocket of his suitcoat. Part of me would always be with him. Laurie and I spent a few days dealing with estate issues and then returned home. 1990 came in with a heaviness and things didn't lighten up much as this year progressed.

Tragedy struck locally as well. A local man who had his own excavation business died unexpectedly while operating a piece of equipment. In June, one of our state troopers lost a son in a motor vehicle accident. I wasn't on duty that night but was notified of the accident and went to the hospital to be with this trooper who was a friend. I spent several hours with him as his wife was out of town. In July, a local woman from a Christian camp on the Gunflint Trail was riding her bike and was struck by a vehicle pulling a trailer and died. Later in this same year, two Arrowhead Electric employees were electrocuted in a freak accident up the Gunflint Trail. These victims were well-known people in our community. We grieved along with the community.

In addition, we investigated a fatal plane crash where all three on board were killed. The apparent cause of the accident was something as simple as running out of fuel. We also had a suicide and two more drownings this year.

While all this was occurring, the sheriff's department had been getting a "heads up" from the U.S. Forest Service that a Rainbow Gathering was coming our way in July. I really don't know how to describe what a person being referred to as a Rainbow should represent. They look like old hippies and misfits. There were those who drove Audis and those who were dumpster divers looking for handouts. They claimed to be peaceful and their sacred day was the 4th of July. But there were many who were not peaceful. If you're wondering why they came to Cook County, it is because they gather in federal forests in areas without a large law enforcement presence. They select a different state every year and this year they chose Minnesota. Prior to this gathering, we were receiving information from many different police agencies around the country about criminals from their areas traveling to this Rainbow event.

The Rainbow Gathering was projected to number in the thousands and it did. We suspected there were many bad people in this encampment. We had several planning meetings to coordinate a strategy with forestry personnel. The area they settled in was Barker Lake which was located just off the Honeymoon Trail. This is a forest service road that travels west off the Caribou Trail which is about six miles north of Lutsen. A logging road from the Honeymoon Trail goes south to the Barker Lake area. The Rainbow Gathering site was established by the lake just across the Poplar River. A conservative number was around 10,000-12,000 people.

The sheriff's department obviously didn't have the man-power to control such a large number so we recruited deputies from neighboring Lake and St. Louis counties. There were also several Forest Service law enforcement officers. An incident command post was established at the Village Inn at Lutsen Mountains. Several Rainbow participants attempted to dis-rupt law enforcement efforts to control this gathering. They tried to sabotage a temporary communication tower that had been established. When routine drug traffic checkpoints were set up on Highway 61, they discovered the Barker Lake site could be accessed on the Honeymoon Trail by going up the Sawbill Trail north from Tofte. The Honeymoon Trail runs east and west between the Caribou and Sawbill Trails. When we discovered folks were sneaking in the back door, the Forest Service made the Honeymoon Trail a one-way road and posted an officer at the intersection of the Sawbill Trail and the Honeymoon Road to stop this activity. I was at the Barker Lake site for the duration of the gathering with regular assistance from fellow Cook County deputies. This was an especially stressful period for me as so much else was going on in the county. In addition, I had just lost both my parents four months ago.

These Rainbows seemed unable to obey any law whenever they left their encampment. The jail in Grand Marais was full all the time and the Minnesota State Patrol occupied the entire Cliff Dweller Motel near Tofte. They transported prisoners for us every day to Duluth. Rainbows all had made up names and never gave a straight answer. At one area they claimed as a medical site, I was told their doctor's name was

"Water Running on the Rocks". Their special day was the 4th of July. On that day, they would gather in a large clearing, hold hands and chant. People from this group started showing up in early June and didn't leave until well into July. On July 8th, the camp's security man with the Rainbow name "Badger" notified our office of a body discovered in a wooded area behind one of the kitchens they had assembled. Dave Wirt, a fellow Cook County deputy, went into the camp with me to investigate. As we started walking down the path toward this makeshift kitchen, we walked past many tents pitched just off the trail. When the occupants saw us, they hollered out "guns in church, guns in church!" "What does this remind you of?", I asked Dave. "Medieval times." he replied. That chant of "guns in church" echoed up the trail and acted as a Rainbow phone call. The cops are coming!

We located the body and examined the site. A healthy-looking male body lying face down on a slope with no signs of a wound. We took pictures and turned him over and discovered livor mortis (settling of the blood in the upper body postmortem). Insect activity had eaten away his face and neck. This man was transported to Hennepin County Medical Center and the doctors couldn't come up with a specific cause of death. The toxicology report was negative, and the hyoid bone was missing due to insect activity. The ensuing investigation took quite a bit of time before we could even identify this person. Before a person arrived at the road going to this gathering, their vehicles were parked in a large gravel pit alongside the Caribou Trail. The Rainbows were transported on a trailer from the gravel pit to the gathering site. A backwoods shuttle service. There were hundreds of vehicles in this pit and as people left the gathering, we kept track of the cars still parked there. Eventually, there were only two vehicles that remained and we ran registration checks to determine the owners. That is how we identified our dead person. Once the man was identified, the investigation continued. We located some of the man's property in the possession of other Rainbows and one of this man's credit cards was used in a coffee shop in New York City. I wanted to go to Ohio where our victim was from and attempt to locate a person who may have come to the gathering with him. This was getting to be a lengthy investigation and with so much else going on in our busiest season, I was told by my boss to drop this investigation. Reluctantly, I did even though I received calls from frantic parents whose children told them that they saw terrible things while attending this gathering.

Several Rainbows stayed in the area and chose to hang around in Grand Marais and others seemed to gravitate to the Hovland area where there were some like-minded folks. Very stressful summer!

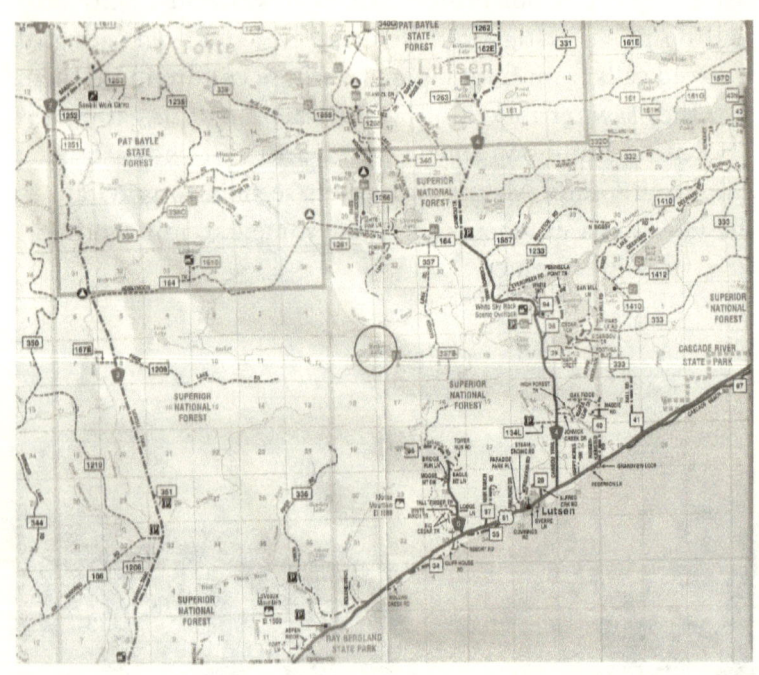

1990 Rainbow Gathering Site

17

MURDER AND MAYHEM

January 1991 came and in addition to the Beargrease Sled Dog Marathon, a new event arrived. The I-500, a snowmobile race from Winnipeg, Canada to St. Paul, Minnesota. The best part of that race was that the racers were in and out of the county in a couple of hours.

Information regarding the Rainbow Gathering continued trickling in for several weeks after the event was over. I had finally learned the identity of the deceased person at the Barker Lake site. Time spent on this case set me back with other cases. I had an intrafamilial sexual assault case and an additional rape case that I was preparing for court.

In addition, I was investigating a burglary in a remote area of the county and had good suspects in mind. Every now and then, investigations are aided by good information received. In this burglary case, I got lucky and the information I received enabled me to establish probable cause for a search warrant. That warrant was executed and stolen property was located. Arrests were made and the property was returned.

I was also working with U.S. Air Guard personnel setting up a remote radar site to determine the volume of suspicious airplane traffic coming from Canada and getting lost in ground clutter once they were over Lake Superior. I suspected this was related to drug trafficking activity. There had been several reports by lodge owners of small aircraft flying over areas of the upper Gunflint Trail both toward Canada and then back toward Lake Superior at treetop level with no lights. This remote surveillance lasted a week and a short time later, we received a report indicating more plane traffic than our observers anticipated seeing. Good information but we really had no resources to respond. We would pass it on to neighboring authorities.

A call from the Gunflint Lodge located 40 miles northwest of Grand Marais up the Gunflint Trail resulted in an interesting case. This lodge has several employees and I had been called to investigate a theft. When a situation like this occurs, I'm inclined to ask questions of the employees who have been recently hired. I interviewed a man who seemed somewhat nervous. He denied stealing anything but, in my opinion, was holding something back. We had a good conversation and I was able to gain his confidence. He told me he had been hanging out with some guys who shot someone. I remember thinking, "Well, this certainly isn't about a theft." He told me he met two guys up the Gunflint Trail who had been employed by a business near Saganaga Lake. These men told him that they had an encounter with a guy on a motorcycle at a gas station in Ashland, Wisconsin. They didn't like a comment he allegedly made and followed the motorcyclist out of the gas station for several miles from Ashland into Michigan. At some point they decided to run him off the road. They smashed into his cycle with their car sending him crashing into a ditch. The cycle rider was injured and sitting along the road when these two men stopped their vehicle, walked over to him and shot him. They covered him and his cycle up with brush and left the scene. I asked the employee if he knew the caliber of the guns used and he told me two specific types. He thought this may have happened somewhere on the south shore of Lake Superior and occurred quite some time ago.

I was a member of the Lake Superior Drug Task Force and shortly after this conversation, I called Bayfield police and asked them if they were aware of any unsolved homicides on the south shore. They said they weren't. A few days later, at a task force meeting, I brought this story up to other members and a Superior, Wisconsin officer said he might know of something. He said he would check a source and get back to me. Later that evening, when I arrived home, I got a phone call from an agent with the Michigan State Police. He asked me what I had going on. I relayed the story my guy had told me and there was a pause on the phone. He asked if I was told what caliber weapon was used and I told him. He said, "We need to talk." As it turned out, the Michigan authorities were investigating this as a cold case.

This murder took place not far from Wakefield, Michigan. It happened May 24, 1990. I and my informant met with the Michigan State Police in Duluth, Minnesota and this investigation began. It was quite lengthy and involved several trips to Duluth, Carlton County, rural St. Louis County and Michigan. I served two search warrants to recover information on the vehicle used in this crime. One was to locate the vehicle which was in rural Carlton County. I interviewed the employee there and he remembers gunshell casings on the floor of the vehicle before he towed it away to a junkyard. The second warrant was used to locate the vehicle at the junkyard. Records at the junkyard revealed that the car had been crushed but documents showed the vehicle belonged to the alleged suspect. The records of the crushed vehicle included the license plate of this car. That information was given to the Michigan authorities and they ran an off-line computer search of this plate number. That is a process that allows the tracking of a vehicle when that license plate is run anywhere by an officer. This off-line search showed this particular plate had been run by a police officer on the night of the murder. The shooters had damaged a tire when they ran the victim off the road. They parked at a gas station in a small town not far from the scene waiting for it to open so they could fix their tire. While they were parked, a police officer noticed their vehicle. He stopped and had a brief conversation with the occupants and ran their license plate. This police action put the shooters near the scene during the same time period as the murder and was a great aid to the investigation. Michigan authorities also located a gun that had been thrown in Lake Superior off a dock in Ashland, Wisconsin. These suspects were from Wrenshall and the Duluth area. The trial started in April 1992. It took place in Crystal Falls, Michigan. The first suspect was convicted in this trial of 2nd degree murder. At a later trial, the second suspect was also convicted of 2nd degree murder. In addition, we solved cases of arson in Carlton County, a stolen vehicle in Lake County, and a burglary in Ashland which they committed.

Late June in 1991, I went to Grand Portage on a follow-up investigation. The case involved an employee who worked for the charter boat captain we arrested in my "Busted" chapter, the money laundering drug operation. This fellow had given a statement earlier to us regarding this case, then gave a different version to a federal grand jury. A federal agent and I had an arrest warrant for perjury and we were going to take him into custody. When we located him and told him he was under arrest, this well-built man looked stunned, became pale and passed out. I never had that happen before. In July, I transported this man to federal court in St. Paul.

Chief Deputy Dick Dorr

A call that the sheriff's department received in the fall of 1990 was an attempt to locate a young man who took off from the St. Cloud area after getting involved in activity he thought was worse than it actually was. It was reported that he was coming to our county. His vehicle was located on a forestry road four miles west of Grand Marais. There was no sign of him at this time and the vehicle was removed. The following spring, a man who had purchased some property nearby, was walking in the woods. At a location in his woods that offered a scenic view, he found this young man. He had shot himself while sitting on the edge of this vista and fell several feet onto a ledge. I and members of our Search &

Rescue team responded to this location. It was a very difficult recovery due to nature's elements and the difficulty of getting onto the ledge he was on. I was thankful that one of our team volunteered to drop down to the ledge and begin the process of retrieving this young victim of an apparent suicide. We located a weapon at the site. I had a son the same age as this young man and this case really bothered me. Dealing with young people who think they may be in more trouble than they actually are can make for unpredictable outcomes.

In April of 1991, we received information that four juveniles, two of them runaways, were coming to Cook County in two separate vehicles. They were headed to a cabin in a remote area near Hovland. One of the young men had a relative that owned this particular cabin. There was still snow on the ground and when we checked the road in to this cabin, there was no evidence of a vehicle entering. Highway 61 was being watched for the vehicles and at one point, a state trooper stopped one of the cars and was informed the car with the two runaways had made it to this cabin in the early morning hours. The runaways told their friends they would shoot any police that tried to follow them. I and several officers from our department, state and tribal conservation officers and state patrolmen located the runaways' vehicle at the entrance to a long road leading to their cabin. We proceeded up the road in off-road vehicles, stopped short of the cabin and secured the perimeter of the building. We called for them to come out peacefully and, in a few minutes, they complied. They had a shotgun and several knives but offered no resistance. This was one occasion I can recall having plenty of backup. Multiple agency cooperation was always appreciated.

Cook County deputy Dick Dorr loads his carbine before going up the Hovland Fire Tower Road to the cabin occupied by two teenagers considered armed and dangerous. At his feet are fresh snowmobile tracks left by the two boys.

In 1991, a sexual assault case I was investigating went to trial July 11th. On July 12th, a fire at Windigo Lodge 30 miles up the Gunflint Trail burned the lodge to the ground. The fire consumed the building immediately and some people were able to jump from the second- and third-floor windows. The lodge owner and his mother-in-law perished along with five others who were staying there. The lodge owner's wife got out. This was a major incident for deputies and first responders. Searching in the debris was a very difficult task.

The fire occurred on the 12th and the rape case resumed on the 15th of July. A jury acquitted the man charged with rape in this case. It seems to me, if there is no physical evidence in cases like this, it turns into "he said, she said". I always believed the victim. Why would anyone make up something like that? Sounds naive on my part, but after many years of dealing with victims, I felt I was a pretty good judge of character.

No shortage of investigations took me into 1992. Once again, there was the good old Beargrease Sled Dog Marathon to start the year. A suicide at Lutsen Mountain took place in late January. A group of young people from the Twin Cities rented a multi-level townhouse. A 22-year-old member of this group went to the lower level and shot himself in the head with a .45 caliber semi-automatic pistol. When he pulled the trigger, he fired a quick second round through the ceiling and the bullet went up into the area where his friends were. This bullet glanced off a piece of furniture, then grazed the leg of a male friend and continued up to the third level of the building. It struck the ceiling and we located the bullet on the bed upstairs. Fortunately, no one was struck any worse than the glancing blow by the second shot. What goes on in the mind of a young man that causes him to separate from his friends, go to a dark lower level in a rented townhouse and shoot himself while the party goes on upstairs? There is no good answer and sometimes it just pisses me off.

The last couple of years have been very heavy with personal loss in our community and in my life. The next couple of cases may not have been as tragic as some but were very disappointing to say the least. One case involved a burglary where a safe was taken out of the home. I knew this owner and felt I had some pretty good suspects. Several leads didn't pan out and no one was arrested. One of those cases where "knowing and proving" are two different things. Very close to the same time, another friend had his home entered and a very substantial amount of cash was taken. Once again,

I thought there was a good suspect and we conducted two search warrants. We came up empty.

Meanwhile other deputies were also kept very busy. It seemed as though a lot of negative things were happening. I was glad to see the end of 1992 approaching. At this point in my career, I was always uneasy on New Years Eve. In the past I have had to arrest several locals for driving offenses like DWI. Four of those were guys I played football with, and one was the best man in my wedding. Some nights the stress levels were much higher. I really came to dislike special event weekends.

18

HUMBLED

The last three months of 1992 included the second trial of a suspect in the Michigan murder case. That involved a trip back to Michigan. This suspect was eventually convicted of murder. After this trial I had an opportunity to meet the parents of the victim who thanked me for my efforts in solving the case. That is always a powerful moment filled with emotion.

In November, I assisted the Grand Marais police in making an arrest. The chief was following up on information he received regarding a man with a young girl checking into a local motel who looked suspicious. He discovered this fellow had kidnapped his daughter from the child's mother in a domestic dispute case. We went to the motel and arrested this man and took the child into protective custody. She was transported to Duluth and plans were made for her mother to pick her up.

Later in the same month, the sheriff's department assisted the Grand Marais police locating a missing local woman.

Friends reported they couldn't locate her and were concerned as she was depressed. We found her lying along a city street in cold, rainy weather. We took her to the local hospital and she eventually made a nice recovery, both physically and emotionally.

In December, one of our deputies was called to investigate a murder-suicide. This case involved a married couple. The woman was a school bus driver and well known in the county. These kinds of calls are always a shock to a community, especially when locals are involved. They are very stressful to investigate.

In February '93, an unusual call came in. A tanker truck caught on fire in the Tofte area along Highway 61. The fire was so high and intense that it destroyed overhead phone lines and disrupted telephone connections for a large number of people. Just when you think you've seen it all. This turned into a busy month as the truck fire call was followed by another criminal sexual misconduct investigation. A few days later we served a search warrant for drugs at a residence in Schroeder.

In May, the parents of the young man who died during the Rainbow Gathering three years earlier, drove from Ohio and asked me to show them where their son was found. The father was a judge and I was thinking of some of the questions he might ask about his son's death. Many survivors look for some kind of explanation. The parents seemed content to see the location and didn't ask questions pertaining to the investigation that took place. A specific cause of death had never been established in this case. I hated to return to that Barker Lake area due to all the stressful memories of that gathering.

In June, we actually had a lighter family moment as our oldest son, Mitchell, graduated from high school. He and his classmates were excellent students and good athletes. During this last school year, they enjoyed many successes in athletics and several of the boys were being recruited to play college football. That was fun and exciting. Mitch ended up at the University of Minnesota, Morris campus. He played a year of football, a season of baseball, and ended up as a student assistant basketball coach.

Due to sightings of what some Grand Portage residents described as suspicious activity on Lake Superior, our Lake Superior Drug Task Force brought their boat up the North Shore. We were going to launch and patrol the area around the Susie Islands and Pigeon River off the Grand Portage coast for unusual activity. We did launch our boat, but the sea was too rough to board another boat so the plan was scrapped.

Later in the year, I and a forestry LEO (Law Enforcement Officer) located a remote marijuana garden and placed sensors around the site. This site was a logging road located off of a U.S. forestry road known locally as the Bally Creek Road. It just so happened this logging road was a favorite of mine and one I had hunted grouse on for many years with my dad, my wife, my sons and grandsons. The sensors we used belonged to the forest service and represented more technology that the sheriff's department didn't have. These sensors would emit a sound if this site was visited. We did respond to a sensor alarm and caught some locals coming out of the patch, but the men we checked hadn't harvested anything yet and had nothing in their possession. Now that they knew we were aware of this grow, we pulled the plants.

Working bailiff duty, continuing investigations that seemed never-ending and prisoner transports took care of the balance of 1993.

1993 and 1994 would rank as some of my toughest years. I had fought anxiety in the past and felt I was dealing fairly well with negative influences. Alcohol was something I hadn't taken into consideration. Whenever I felt my use of it getting away from me, I tried to back off. I'm smart enough to know that medicating myself after a stressful shift wasn't always the best way to deal with things. I would quit for periods of time and then start up again. Yet, I wasn't pulling the wool over my wife's eyes, even if I thought so.

One day I came home after a shift, huffing and puffing up our deck stairs. Laurie recognized the physical symptoms I exhibited such as shortness of breath and fatigue along with my weight gain. She decided I needed to be checked out by a doctor. We went to the hospital and after a brief exam, I had an EKG (electrocardiogram) taken. It showed I was in atrial fibrillation, an irregular heart rhythm. My chest was filling with fluid causing shortness of breath and weight gain. I was given a diuretic and lost 15-20 pounds of fluid overnight. An appointment with a cardiologist in Duluth was made.

The a-fib (atrial fibrillation) diagnosis was confirmed and they decided to cardiovert me using the electronic paddles. Prior to zapping me, they did an angiogram to make sure there were no blockages in my arteries. They threaded a very small catheter into my femoral artery and manipulated it into my heart. Then, dye was released to check for blockages. None was found and they performed the cardioversion procedure later the same day. Doctors used a defibrillator in an attempt to return my heart to a normal rhythm. It didn't work! I was told my atrium was too enlarged and basically wasn't going to cooperate. In a conference afterwards with the cardiologist, he told me there were only a few reasons for this condition to occur in someone my age with an otherwise athletic heart. One of the reasons could be alcohol consumption. "How much do you drink?" When I saw the look on my wife's face as he spoke, I realized the pain I had caused in our life. That was the day I quit drinking! I remember when I quit smoking at age 30 how difficult that was. A physical addiction. That seemed like nothing compared to admitting something like alcohol can sneak up on you and get the better of you. A psychological addiction? I was put on various heart strengthening medications and sent home. I took some time off before returning to work, 30 pounds lighter and hopefully with a better attitude.

I recall some cases in 1994 with sadness and frustration. A suicide case reminded me that it is so difficult to come up with plausible explanations. I was called to an area near Paradise Beach on a secluded site by Lake Superior. A young man who worked with youth in the community and was highly regarded, took his life with a gun. This was the kind of victim I would have loved to have had a chance to interdict with. Standing over this young man, I felt such sadness looking down at the devastation and then up at the incredible beauty of the lake and surroundings. Sometimes, I just felt helpless. I met his family a few days later, his mom, dad, and brother. Such a nice family. Everything I learned about this victim never led anywhere near suicide. The mystery of this type of solution just got deeper for me. Having sons of my own gave me some insight into the pain these parents were feeling.

Another frustrating case was a cabin burglary on a lake 30 miles up the Gunflint Trail. The cabin, located on a lovely small lake, belonged to an older couple. While they were away, burglars entered and took furniture and many household items. Several of the items taken were very special to them. These types of burglaries usually occurred in late fall after cabin owners left to winter elsewhere or early spring before owners returned to their cabins. I contacted several police agencies in northern Minnesota and alerted them of the burglary. I requested they check area pawn shops. Unfortunately, stolen property doesn't always turn up at a pawn shop. I didn't get a response. Due to the volume of theft going on, most police agencies simply don't have the officers to dedicate to this type of incident. Sometimes, you just have to get lucky. In this case, we did. A few days later, I received a call from the cabin owner saying he and his wife were in Duluth and when they walked past a secondhand store, they saw some of their furniture in the window. Amazing luck! I drove to Duluth and went to this store. The manager gave me the name of the fellow who brought these items to him. I checked with the Duluth Police Department and discovered this man was an active burglar. I obtained a search warrant for this man's house and executed it with the assistance of a Duluth detective. We recovered several more items from the cabin burglary. I had the cabin owners on the phone and would describe an item as I found it. In retrospect, I should have had them with me. Now the frustrating part! The burglars left no physical evidence such as fingerprints at the scene of the cabin break-in in Cook County. In addition, our suspect was in jail on other charges. And when I questioned him, he denied having anything to do with this theft. I always thought just having possession of the property should have been enough, but not in Minnesota. No charges were filed on this suspect.

Another call came from Grand Portage and involved a man who was found deceased in a room at the Grand Portage Lodge. I talk about that in Chapter 14 involving unusual cases. That case involved a victim who was very highly regarded in the medical profession and left many wondering why. In many cases we worked, there always seemed to be questions with no answers. A lot of frustration.

There were many trips out of the county during this time period. Task force meetings, drug investigation seminars in Bemidji, Minnesota and an unusual number of prisoner transports. My longest trip in 1994 was a drive to Marshall, Minnesota to investigate a sex crime. The statute of limitations had expired and prevented a case from being made.

One major decision was made after much thought. I was going to run for sheriff in the November election. I don't recall when I announced it, but it was early enough to spark plenty of conversation. I was the only deputy not protected by the union and some of the talk was whether or not I would get fired for running against my boss. That didn't happen and a short time later, two more deputies filed. I was new to the political side of things, but I always felt fairly good about the way I interacted with citizens. There are always those who don't care for you and there isn't much you can do about that. I just wanted the sheriff's department to start going in a different direction. The campaigning was civil among the officers and if anyone made a mistake, it was me. I sent out flyers requesting financial support for the campaign. I discovered that is not something you do in Cook County. I lost in the primary to Dave Wirt and the sheriff. We three challengers pooled our support and Dave was elected sheriff. I took this defeat better than I thought I might. I felt it was time for new leadership.

19

DEPARTURE

The 1994 election had taken place and a new sheriff had been voted in. And, it wasn't me. I had no particular thought other than I hadn't planned on losing. I made some political decisions along the way that worked against me, and I thought I was prepared to deal with whatever the future held. I'm not sure I was. I don't recall how many days had gone by since Dave Wirt, the newly elected sheriff, took over, but it wasn't long before he and I had a meeting in his office.

Sheriff Wirt informed me he would be appointing a new chief deputy. That is something you must prepare for if you enter the political arena. The winner of the election controls the outcome. I was demoted from chief deputy to patrol deputy, and a new man would take over as chief deputy. Awkward as that could have been, everyone liked Mark Falk, the new chief deputy, including me.

The new sheriff was actually going to give his chief deputy administrative responsibilities, something my former job title implied but never happened. It didn't seem that I would be losing my investigating opportunities, but I was losing $10,000 a year in salary. That is one more thing you had better be ready to accept if you lose an election.

Needless to say, I was in a bit of a funk this year. Calls kept coming in and eventually, I was off and running. A very sad suicide call from Grand Portage came in. That incident was documented in my "Unusual Calls" chapter. Two more calls to Grand Portage involved backing up a fellow deputy on a domestic call and then investigating a sawmill fire up there. Later in January of '95, I met with the fire marshall who was investigating this fire. Cause of this fire was inconclusive.

A prisoner transport to Grand Rapids and another to Carlton County kept me on the road. A few days later another trip to Grand Rapids for a drug refresher school followed by an intoxilyzer refresher school in Duluth.

The winter stayed busy. I responded to Grand Portage on another domestic call. I arrested a male and locked him up charging him with assault. A few shifts later, I was called to Lutsen to assist a victim of an obscene phone call. In some cases like this, a suspect can be developed by information a victim may have regarding who he or she has been in recent contact with. After a short investigation, this obscene caller was identified and the victim agreed to a written letter of apology. In June, I was busy preparing for a court trial that involved a man who had transported drugs into Cook County. In what seemed like a continuous number of tragic events, I assisted the Grand Marais police with a suicide. A single man living alone along County Road 7 took his life with a gun.

August continued to be very busy. Saganaga Lake, at the end of the Gunflint Trail experienced a forest fire in an area called the Corridor, a narrow waterway that went from the boat landing into the main body of the lake. A fire can jump long distances due to hot embers drifting in the gusts of wind that the fire itself creates. I was in a boat on Sag with a conservation officer keeping folks out of a problem area and providing security for cabins. There was a large presence of firefighters. They are impressive to watch. After a few days, they had this fire under control. The danger is great when it gets so dry that evergreens just explode when fire hits them. Many resources go into fighting these fires and the U.S. Forestry's logistical skills always impressed me.

In the Fall of this year, two Grand Marais police officers were investigating burglaries in town and had identified suspects and where the stolen property was located. I helped them draft a search warrant for an apartment where this property was alleged to be. We executed the warrant and found a substantial amount of stolen goods. More Information was gathered by these officers that led us to another residence and more property was found. It was fun helping these young police officers.

This was a busy year with lots of calls to Grand Portage and the Gunflint Trail. Towards the end of a shift sometime after 02:00 am, a local doctor had a psyche patient that had to be taken to Duluth, so I was on the road at 02:45 am. Another 15-hour shift. A couple days later, at 03:45 am, I was called to an accident that happened very close to the hospital entrance. A fellow was driving down the Gunflint Trail and the driver of a logging truck was going up the Gunflint to start his day. The fellow coming down was intoxicated and struck the logging truck head on. The driver of the car went through the windshield and was spreadeagled face down on the center line of the road. This man lived but required lifetime assistance at a care facility as a result of this accident. Fortunately, the truck driver wasn't injured.

There seemed to be a lot of different types of incidents these last couple years. Perhaps I noticed this more because I was a road officer again. One day I was in a remote county location with social services interviewing youngsters. Another day I was assisting the state patrol on a traffic stop. I was also serving papers or responding to domestics.

One late July evening, a young woman requested an officer come to her cabin two miles east of Grand Marais along Highway 61. She was in her cabin alone watching television. There was a window off to her left side and she caught the image of a person looking at her. She got up and called the office. I was less than two minutes away but at night, the "peeper" must have seen my headlights when I was responding and he fled. The victim told me that she tried to appear calm when she called the office so she wouldn't spook him. The peeper had been standing outside looking at this woman through the window and masturbating. Too bad we didn't have DNA capabilities at this time. He left a sample on the siding! Another first for me!

Next, a call requested a deputy to respond to the Lutsen area. A young, possibly suicidal woman was in crisis, and I responded. We had a long talk and she eventually agreed to go with me to our hospital and then to Duluth for some help. I saw this woman in town a few weeks later and she was very thankful. That always felt good.

A call that probably could be put into the unusual file took place one afternoon on Kadunce River, a stream flowing into Lake Superior nine miles east of Grand Marais. Near the mouth of this river there is a shale rock wall forming a ledge several feet high. This rock wall protrudes and offers footholds to perhaps tempt someone to try and scale the ledge. On this particular day, a mother and her two daughters thought they would give it a try. Part way up, they discovered the sharpness and instability of this type of rock. The office received a call for help and I responded. I and a man at the scene walked up the bank of the stream and stopped at the top edge of the shale wall. We lowered a rope to help the women off the wall. Happy ending. No Injuries.

Late in summer, I was called to a drowning at Temperance River near the west end community of Tofte, another North Shore river with a waterfall into a pool. A father, his 15-year-old son and a 14-year-old friend were in the pool below this waterfall. Suddenly, the 14-year-old friend was pulled under and drowned. It took some time for a recovery. When I was interviewing the father and his son, they were in shock. They said, "He was right next to us!" That is exactly how fast accidents happen. This grief-stricken family friend had to go home and explain what happened to some heartbroken parents. North Shore streams are rugged and dangerous. We've lost people in several of them. Sitting with these survivors gave insight into how traumatic this is. Minutes of fun turned into a devastating accident in just seconds. That is part of the reason I became overly cautious with my own family. Watching all this constant heartbreak is difficult.

There was a period in the last few months of 1996 that was spent on continuing education seminars such as "Interviewing Child Victims". This was sponsored by First Witness, a specialized training center in Duluth, Minnesota. Then, I attended a drug eradication class in Grand Marais and "Blue Lightning Training" sponsored by U.S. Customs. That authorized deputies to assist with U.S. customs enforcement.

In the last week of January, 1997, the sheriff's department received a complaint of criminal sexual misconduct. The reported incident was allegedly committed by an individual toward a child victim. I was informed this suspect was on probation for similar offenses and this was also a probation violation. I contacted the probation officer and was advised to pick this person up. I locked the alleged offender up and began a very lengthy investigation. The victim was a baby so I felt I had to do the best I could to gather enough facts to support these charges.

Three days later, while on a night shift, another call came in that took me to the Village Inn at Lutsen. A man followed his girlfriend to work and brought their domestic issues with him. I responded and found the party in an office area. He was intoxicated and would not listen to reason. I arrested him for disorderly conduct and wrestled him into a position to be handcuffed. A police officer drove from Grand Marais to assist and we took the man to jail.

I spent a considerable amount of time over the next few months investigating the child abuse case. The alleged perpetrator had been living in a home in Grand Portage where there was a baby. His probation prohibited him from being alone with a child. Previously, he had lived in Duluth. When I checked with Duluth Police, I found he had an extensive record of similar offenses. This case was reported by social services after a doctor discovered this baby had injuries that could have only been caused by specific sexual activity. That doctor's opinion was also supported by another medical professional. My job was to try and determine if there was a window of time that this suspect was left alone with this child. I advised the county attorney that I thought this was an appropriate case to introduce "Spreigl" evidence. Previous bad acts seemed to fit this scenario. After interviewing several people in Grand Portage, I felt a window of opportunity had been established for this crime to have been committed.

January and February seemed very busy with many calls and even though there was a lot going on, I tried to give the criminal sexual misconduct investigation priority. March 21st, I went to Duluth to discuss medical information with a doctor regarding this case. I was also attempting to locate and interview witnesses and past victims.

On March 28th, 1997, I went to the courthouse in Grand Marais and engaged in friendly conversation with the personnel director. I don't recall how we got on the subject, but

I was sharing how I'd been talking to a former classmate of mine who had been a St. Louis County deputy sheriff. He told me he had recently taken a PERA (Public Employees Retirement Association) retirement due to the fact he was taking blood thinners. He had been injured in Vietnam and suffered from blood clots in his leg. I said to the personnel director, "Heck, I've been taking blood thinners for three years because of atrial fibrillation." The director said "Well Dick, it's one thing for you to know what you have and be willing to work with it. It's another thing for me to know what you have and be willing to let you work with it. I think you need to go home." That was the first day of my retirement. My last case would have to be concluded by someone else.

I took my badge and gun off that day and, since then, have spent many hours thinking about that conversation. My reaction was similar to how I felt after the election defeat. First, the defeat, then the salary reduction and now the job itself. It never occurred to me to enter a legal battle over the loss of health benefits which, as I look back, I probably should have done. At age 49, I went home wondering what the future had in store.

20

NEW BEGINNINGS

So now, what do I do? While I thought about the future, the first order of business would be to use up the comp time and sick leave I had on the books. That would provide my typical take-home pay for close to six months. During that time, I'd figure out my retirement income from PERA. I was made aware of a retirement party being planned by the sheriff's department staff with input from my wife. That did take place at the Harbor Light Supper Club and was very well attended. I was presented with my service pistol, a model 1911 .45 semi-automatic pistol. It was very touching for me to see the various community people who showed up. Stories were shared along with a lovely meal.

Three years ago, I lost an election many told me I was certain to win. Next, due to a medical issue, I was released from my job after 26 years, a job I felt I was good at. I always felt there was a particular way to do this type of job especially in a small community you intended to stay in for an entire career. It was 1997 and there was a lot to think about. My oldest son, Mitchell, would be spending the next year student teaching in New Zealand. Richie, our youngest, was graduating from high school and would be off to Fergus Falls Community College in August. Laurie, my wife, was working as a nurse in the local hospital. From a financial standpoint, things didn't seem too bad as we had managed to pay off our mortgage over the twenty years we lived in town on West 7th Avenue. We opted to put me on Laurie's medical insurance which was significant since I was only 49 years old. My PERA disability retirement didn't equal what I had been making while working but it was pretty close.

I don't recall when Grand Marais became the home of its own radio station, WTIP. However, in 1993, I and a former football teammate of mine began a volunteer career broadcasting football and basketball games. We traveled to all the football games and several of the basketball contests. My partner was the play-by-play guy, I was the color guy. We received a lot of positive feedback from community listeners. When you live in a remote location like Grand Marais, it is nice to have the games brought home over the radio. We saw

a lot of the state together and met a lot of great people. It was a special time in my life. It included being able to broadcast state tournament games from the Metrodome in Minneapolis when several Cook County teams went to the state tourney. I had an opportunity to see both of my sons play there.

Next, came a term on the school board. During this period of time, two former students I had gone to school with were the principal and superintendent of Cook County High. Also, a former teacher of all three of us was a fellow board member. My tenure as a board member lasted one term. I began investigating how money from volunteer groups was being handled. I didn't care for how the process was being conducted and was vociferous about it during a board meeting. The group I was raising questions with left that meeting and recruited someone to run against me in the next election. They did and I lost another election.

At the end of 1998, Mitch, our oldest son, came home having graduated with a teaching degree and coaching certificate.

Jane and her "kids"

Seven former students of Jane Mianowski's were in close enough proximity to the superintendents office last week to be caught for a picture with their high school math teacher. Standing from left to right: Elementary principal Chuck Futterer, school board member Dick Dorr, Special Education Secretary Sherryl Thompson, Administrative Assistant Cindy Carpenter, Superintendent's Secretary Kathleen Johnson, Business Manager Dorothy Eliasen and Superintendent Dale Tormondsen. Seated is Mianowski, who still volunteers at the district schools to tutor children in math.

He secured a teaching position in Grand Marais and lived in town with us for almost one year. Earlier in the 90s, Laurie and I had obtained some acreage four miles west of town along County Road 7. We decided to build on this land and sell our home in town to Mitch. We began the planning and building project and in July 1999, we moved into our new home. We had 16 acres on part of an old farm site that had both a lovely field and a large wooded area. Mitch took over the house in town and continued his teaching career. Rich left Fergus Falls and decided to go job hunting. We were busy learning how to live in the country and take care of a large property. I had a local man dig a pond with a plan to put fish in it. I also discovered how long it could take to mow several acres. Next, came sodding for a large lawn area and planting several evergreens. While we were at it, why not try our hand at gardening. There were also the raspberry plants we brought from town. This was turning into a lot of upkeep.

During the building, a good friend worked with me on the interior of the home preparing lots of tongue and groove paneling. Laurie and I brushed many feet of paneling with polyurethane. When we discovered how much equipment one needs to keep this type of property going, another garage was added. All these things really kept us busy. Plus, Laurie was still working. There was one more large addition to our adventure. A mortgage! After being free of that for several years, it was an eye opener, especially with medical insurance added in.

The following years seemed to fly by. Laurie continued her job as a nurse until major back surgery ended her career. She recovered and transitioned to being a "HUC" (Hospital Unit Coordinator). She has great organizational skills. Meanwhile, I worked with a friend who introduced me to the Firewise Program. This was a state sponsored job to assist rural property owners with suggestions on how to make forested properties safer from fire. I also volunteered at the Superior National Golf Course as a ranger, someone who keeps the pace of play up. In exchange, I was able to play there. That led to a couple of summers mowing for them as well. Every Fall came football and basketball seasons and the radio gig. Mitch started out as a football assistant coach and girls' basketball coach. He built the girls program into a very good one. After a few years, they went to state. Richie was in a relationship and began employment with a large, commercial industrial company. They purchased a house in Blaine, Minn.

Laurie worked at her HUC position until September 2007. Prior to that time, even though there was health insurance for her at work, my portion was getting pretty expensive. We sought less expensive insurance options. After she retired from the HUC position, she followed what had always been her first love-pharmacy. She became a certified pharmacy technician and worked for the local drug store. I took a part time job cleaning at the Catholic church and delivering medications for the drug store.

During those years that flew by, Mitch got married to a college sweetheart. He eventually left the girls basketball program and became the head football coach. We assisted him and his wife in getting into some property next to us in the country and they built a home where they raised four children, three boys and a girl. Sharing our lives with the grandchildren from diapers to college age were some of the richest years we experienced. The boys, Adam, Jacob and Paul, fished Devils Track Lake with Grandpa and enjoyed deer hunting and also hunting for grouse. Our granddaughter, Rachel, had a lot of kitchen time with Grandma and caught a couple of nice walleyes too. Bonbons at Christmas became a tradition. Richie and his girlfriend separated but he kept the home in Blaine and continues working in the construction and landscaping field.

I tried to write this story of my career a year or so after leaving the job. I brought my career home in boxes of daily logs from the job. They contained the activities of a working shift, day by day, month by month, year by year. Twenty-six years in boxes. I think the reason I backed off at the time was that I just wasn't ready to go there, even though I always thought it was important for Cook County citizens to know some of the history that occurred in the county over the years. Some of the memories were too dark to revisit. As time went on, Laurie said, "You really should do something with all those boxes." So, I started reading them and it lit my fire once again.

Going through the daily logs, there were so many contacts with people that it would be impossible to talk about all of them. So many assists, whether it was giving a ride, opening a locked door, or listening while people shared their deepest secrets with you. That is probably the answer to my biggest questions about how I felt after losing the sheriff's election. I felt I had wound myself into the fabric of the community and was disappointed my efforts didn't seem enough. Then, I was just sent home. It is ironic that when I came to Grand Marais I was the "new kid" in my class. Most of my classmates left the community to work elsewhere but, the "new kid" stayed and grew roots.

How did we end up in Hutchinson, Minnesota after a 54-year marriage spent in Grand Marais? In 2021, Mitchell had an opportunity to advance his career in the southern Minnesota community of Jordan as an elementary school principal. He and I talked over his options and he felt a move was right for him and his wife, Sharon, and the kids. Sharon had been employed at a title company in Grand Marais. Her job was Title Examiner/Title Production. She was able to keep the same employment with their move. Of course, when they left, Paul and Rachel were still in school and made the move with them. Laurie and I realized our next-door support system was no longer there and our large property was getting more difficult to maintain. We missed having them close.

Mitch worked at Jordan for a year and decided to look for a bigger challenge. He applied and was hired as athletic director at Cold Spring Rocori High School. He, Sharon, and Rachel moved to the nearby community of St. Joseph. Sharon was able to make a lateral transfer for her job. Adam graduated from Hillsdale College in Michigan, Jacob is attending college at University of Mary in Bismarck, ND, Paul is attending Benedictine College in Atchison, KS and Rachel is a senior at St. Cloud Cathedral. Rich is maintaining his home in Blaine, a Minneapolis suburb. Laurie and I decided that Hutchinson is almost equal distance from both sons, an hour or so each way. In addition, Laurie is from a small town near "Hutch" and has quite a bit of family here. So, here we are after all this time. I still have some unresolved feelings about how my career came to a screeching halt. Perhaps by letting folks know a little about this law enforcement path I took, I'm still "chasing justice".

21
REFLECTIONS

So, there it is, a look back on a life and career in law enforcement. Maybe most of the job seemed to center around negative events, but the fact is we were usually dealing with people in crisis.

As this chapter is titled, it reflects on a career that perhaps shouldn't have happened. I may have been a bigger than average, rough-looking man, but my strong suit was always compassion. That came through when I was dealing with people in severe crisis. I think my boss and some officers saw that as a weakness. Perhaps that personal conflict I was dealing with evolved into the anxiety I experienced in those years. I laugh when I remember a therapist suggested I might have considered a social worker occupation instead. I know I always hated going to work thinking I may have to arrest another friend or put someone I knew in a body bag. Toward the end of this adventure, my wife's intervention literally saved my life. Now in retirement, I'm able to share my story with you.

As a family, we did have lighter moments and an opportunity to make many friends in the community. Below, I've listed some of the things we shared as a family over the years that brought us joy. I finished with the one big trip that we took and all that it entailed. Even though a lot didn't go as planned, the boys still remember it as a great adventure.

In the 1970s and 80s, Laurie and I took every opportunity to enjoy outings with friends and family. Special dining was available at restaurants. Our favorites were the Happy Fisherman in the Colville area, Pete's Steakhouse at Paradise Beach, the Birch Terrace, and the Viking Room at the East Bay Hotel.

Outdoor activities were also enjoyed. Early in our marriage, we went fishing together. We concentrated on catching walleyes and fished the spots in Devil Track Lake where I used to fish with my dad. Laurie could fillet a fish with the best of them and was a wonderful cook when it came to fish or grouse. When our sons came along, she gave up her place in the boat and the boys joined me. Both Mitch and Rich loved fishing and hunting.

We walked logging roads hunting for grouse in the Fall. To this day, I remember the logging trail we went on. The fall of the year is one of my favorite times and the woods gave off the intoxicating fall aroma. "Nature's perfume" Our first outings were quite successful and, once again, were special to me because this area was where my dad took me as a youngster.

We found time for Cub Scouts, Little League, parades, family reunions, Valley Fair, and Apple Valley Zoo. Laurie made the kids great costumes, incredible birthday cakes and was always there for us. She is truly the most selfless person I know. With Laurie and I both working shift work, one of us was usually home for the boys.

When the boys entered ages nine through fourteen, they became active in Little League baseball. These were special times for me as I was their coach. The practices gave me an opportunity to watch them interact with their teammates and an opportunity to get to know these youngsters. It was a great distraction from stress at work. I can remember putting players who weren't starters into a game and watching their eyes light up when they made a play. I always tried to be encouraging and as these kids grew into adults, several of them told me they had fond memories of the time they played.

As young teens, our sons also participated in school sports. Football and basketball were their favorites. Laurie and I supported these events and while doing so, got to know and become friends with the parents of their teammates. In 1983, the school was dealing with budget issues and talk always involved program cuts. I and five other parents gathered and formed the Cook County Booster Club. We had many fundraisers through the years and, two years in a row, had the Minnesota Vikings in Grand Marais to play a group we called the Cook County All Stars. At a later date, sometime in the 1990s, the club designed a sports calendar with high school sports schedules. We sold ads to local businesses to be put on this calendar and it became a $9,600 fundraiser every spring. Many great parents became involved in this Booster Club and it is still going strong. As the football and basketball seasons came, we made many trips following the kids. Our boys were players on football teams that went to State and played in the Metrodome. A lot of these kids were the same ones that we got to know when they played Little League baseball. During football season, Laurie would feed the team a big pasta meal before home games. That started a tradition among parents.

The Cook County Schools Booster Club elected its Governing Body at their first annual meeting. Seated in a semi-circle from left to right are, Miriam Horen, Sally Eliasen, Dick Crosby, Dick Dorr, Al Heidebrink, Janet Lang and Chris McClure.

As girlfriends and other interests came along for the boys, Laurie and I enjoyed the local bowling alley. I was in a couple of leagues. We especially enjoyed our mixed doubles league on Sunday evening. Sadly, the bowling alley is no more. Those were great times.

Trips to visit friends and family were always enjoyed. And then there was the TRIP!

THE TRIP

I could probably write a book just about our first big family trip. Laurie and I had been dreaming of it, planning it for months, and in 1988, we were actually going. We both had vacation time built up and this trip was starting on Easter break so the kids were not in school. We were going to go first-class in a sleeper car via Amtrak. Our route was south to Texas and then west to Phoenix, Arizona. I had a classmate who lived in the Globe-Miami area, and we were going to tour Arizona and neighboring sites with him and his family. We drove to Apple Valley and stayed at the Country Inn. We got up at 5 am Easter Sunday and had breakfast with friends who drove us to Midway Station to begin our adventure. We waited and waited and waited some more but our train never arrived. We had checked most of our luggage along with my golf clubs and as things turned out, they left and we didn't. We were told the train had engine trouble, hit some poor rail and there was a passenger injury as well. Three hours later, a coach car, the "Empire Builder", finally arrived and we were on our way to Union Station in Chicago. Due to the schedule screw up, they would try to accommodate us with an alternative mode of transportation. At Union Station we were advised we could fly on Southwest to Phoenix that night. I turned that down as I had two tired young boys and a wife who had been up since early morning. Plus, we planned this trip by train because I was not comfortable flying. Plans were to be made the following day by Amtrak officials. We were put up in a nice hotel in downtown Chicago and as I went to bed that night I was wondering where the hell my underwear ended up, not to mention my golf clubs.

In the morning, we went to Union Station and discovered our options had changed, no more offerings of a flight. We were going by train to Flagstaff and it wasn't the southern route, it was through the mountains. I had quit drinking about four months prior to this trip but whiskey was starting to sound good to me. We had four hours to kill before our next train. We walked the bridge over Lake Michigan and several downtown blocks. We were close to the Sears Tower and Laurie thought we should go to the top of this highest building with the view of several states. I was wound pretty tight by then, and having never liked heights in the first place, I declined to go with her. Of course, both boys took my side so Laurie had to go alone. At the time I was still dealing with anxiety issues but in retrospect, I deeply regret not encouraging the boys to join her. Just think, this isn't even the stressful part of the trip yet.

Laurie took the elevator up 110 floors to the top in "sixty seconds" she exclaimed. She enjoyed the views, took some pictures, and joined us for the walk to Union Station to await our train. We lost our first-class accommodations and ended up sitting for two days and nights in a coach car with a woman across the aisle from us who was smoking like a steam engine (pun intended) with two young children laying at her feet. Now I'm going on two and a half days without a fresh change of anything and I did locate the bar car. The boys were unshaken and spent time in the lounge playing games and meeting some travelers.

We arrived in Flagstaff around two in the morning and there was no one there at this mountain outpost station. There were no taxis or services for tourists. A small, empty tour bus was getting ready to pull out of the parking lot and I managed to get the driver's attention and secure a ride down the mountain to Phoenix. The guy driving this bus is college-age and is flying down the road much faster than I felt comfortable going. I told him he didn't have to hurry on our account, but he didn't get the hint. By now I am pissed! All I could think about was getting to Phoenix safely where I knew my friend was waiting for us. Then, I needed to call Amtrak and try to track down our luggage. It must have been around 5am when we rolled into Phoenix and met with Bill, my high school buddy. He drove us to Globe and we rested. I called Amtrak and they gave instructions to buy necessary clothing items, keep the receipts, and they would reimburse me. We got cleaned up and went shopping. I was stressed, Laurie was her usual understanding self, and the kids just thought it was a great adventure. I had spent the better part of the 80s seeing so much misery I just wanted to have a great time and it wasn't happening for me.

The Globe area was developed around a mining operation and my buddy was far up the ladder in this operation. He and his family had taken time off to show us around the entire area. The first leg of our journey was going to be south to the Tucson area and then on to Nogales. We spent a night in a nice motel with a pool in Nogales, Arizona and the next day we ventured into Nogales, Mexico. We ate at Elvira's Mexican restaurant where we were serenaded by mariachi singers and then went shopping and walking around the city. Street vendors and beggars were constantly approaching us. It seemed like a nice afternoon except there were an awful lot of people around. We went into a shop selling Western gear like ropes, belts, hats and items of that nature. I looked around and said," Where is Richie?" Just like that, he was gone. My heart sank! There was Laurie and Mitch, Bill and his wife and two daughters but no Richie! Just as we bolted out to the street, a Mexican man approached us holding Richie by the hand. Richie had been right behind us and apparently didn't see our group go into this store. He just kept walking, turned around and no Mom or Dad. Thank God it turned out well for us!

We returned back to the U.S. and spent another night in the motel at Nogales. Laurie laughed so hard when Richie and I hit the pool with our new swimming trunks that really weren't swimming trunks. I just bought shorts for Richie and didn't realize they weren't lined and they ballooned up in the pool which must have looked hilarious to those who noticed, especially my wife. I called Amtrak and my golf clubs and suitcases had arrived at their Tucson station. We retrieved those items on the way back to Globe where we rested up a couple days before the next leg of our trip.

Ah, what a relaxing trip... A missed train connection, lost luggage, almost three days sitting up in a coach car, three days in the same underwear, a trip from Hell down the side of a mountain and a lost son in Mexico. What could possibly go wrong the rest of the way? I'm wired pretty tight in case you haven't guessed. My wife should be nominated for sainthood!

Next was a trip up to Sedona and Red Rock country. That involves driving up steep mountain roads. My buddy, who is driving, and my two sons and I are in one car. Laurie, Bill's wife Mary and their two daughters are in another car. As they are admiring the views from these goat path roads, I'm white-knuckling it up the side of each mountain pass. We finally got to Sedona and I have to admit it is beautiful country. I think I had been exposed to so much of what goes wrong in life, I found it very difficult to just relax. We drove quite an elevation to stay at Sky Ranch Lodge. I white-knuckled it going up that road too, but we did enjoy the pool and accommodations. We took several pictures with the mountains in the background, it was hard to smile.

The next day it was on to the Grand Canyon. When I first saw that little tear in the earth I was pretty impressed. Of course, my friends and Laurie wanted to take a hike down into the canyon. The path was wide enough for people and the donkeys they could ride into the canyon. When they told me the animals got the inside edge on the trails and the hikers had to go to the outside, I said "Go suck an egg!" or something like that. If you compare a few falls off the cliffs on North Shore rivers, those heights are nothing compared to this canyon. Once again, I'm sure I spoiled another family moment. We spent two days and a night there and both boys caught a stomach virus of some sort. Mitch stayed in bed most of the time and as we were leaving on our next leg of the trip and were pulling out of the lot, Richie threw up in my lap and I caught most of that in my hands. Man, this is relaxing! I recall as we went through Winslow, Arizona enroute to the Hoover Dam, the song "Take It Easy" came to mind.

Onward we go to the dam. That went pretty much without a hitch. It was very impressive as was Roosevelt Lake. We made a brief visit, took several pictures, and then onward to Las Vegas. Bill kept saying how impressive it was in Vegas and how we would be amazed by the Strip. He said we should get there at just about the right time in the evening to see the "lights". As we closed in on the city, all of a sudden it started to rain. We pulled into the lot of Circus-Circus shortly before dark and decided to let the kids have some fun. Adult gambling was on the main floor and games for kids on the upper floor. Bill, who is an expert Blackjack player, stayed downstairs and Laurie and I took the kids to the upper level. There was a game where you tossed a ball through a very small hole to try and win a prize. The ball actually appeared larger than the hole. The man said nobody ever wins the "big moon man" that stood about six feet tall and was a grand prize. Mitch bought three chances and on the first toss, yep, right through the hole. We spent the rest of the trip carrying around this almost six foot, bright orange "moon man".

We went back downstairs and discovered Bill had been winning big. He was about five grand ahead and he wanted Laurie to try her hand at "21". Now, Laurie is Miss Frugal so she found it hard to take two hundred dollars from Bill and play to a minimum bid of twenty dollars. She lost it in a few minutes and we decided it was time to eat. Now, Bill was going to show us the Strip on our way to dinner. Prior to leaving the casino, the rain turned to a downpour and just as we were going outside, lightning knocked out the power and the Strip went black. The only thing I could see was that stupid moon man looking at me in the dark. We made our way to Caeser's Palace and eventually the power came back and we managed to have supper. We spent the night in Las Vegas and took off for Phoenix the next day. The money allotted to us for clothes was at the train station in downtown Phoenix so Bill and I went to pick it up while the girls and kids took off for Globe. We arrived in Phoenix after dark. I went in the station to get the money. There were no people around and the man in the station was behind a counter with bars in front. He was very nervous and said, "You know, we don't usually keep this kind of cash on hand. This is a dangerous part of the city." I thought, "We're only talking a hundred dollars!" I didn't realize you could get your throat slit in that part of town for that amount of money.

We arrived in Globe and spent a couple of days relaxing and playing golf. Bill made arrangements for us to fly home when the time came to leave. The women did some sightseeing which Laurie loved. She fell in love with the desert, the cacti, especially the saguaro. Our hosts were anxious to have us attend a rodeo on the last day of our visit. I'd never been to a genuine rodeo with real cowboys. The day we showed up for the rodeo, the weather turned foul and never got much above the mid-thirties. While watching the rodeo parade in downtown Globe, it hailed! Mary turned to Laurie and said,

"Laurie, it never hails in Globe!" Seemed par for the course to me.

We left for the airport to fly home and at the ticket counter I asked if there would be a problem with our "moon man". The man said, "No, this is a red-eye flight and there are lots of empty seats. The attendant will help you out." So, we get on the plane, and I put "moon man" in an empty seat and the attendant quickly descended on me. "Sir, you cannot put that there!" I explained that the guy at the ticket counter said it shouldn't be a problem and "you would be able to help us out". Well, this wasn't one of the flight attendants this guy was talking about! "Moony" got shoved in a closet in back of the cockpit and we took off for Minneapolis. Of course, I'm still recalling my flight from Hell through the Tetons earlier in the eighties and while my family eventually settles in and falls asleep, I'm wide-eyed and white-knuckling it all the way home. I can't wait to get home to a high-speed chase, something I can control!

POSTSCRIPT

Beneath the Badge

By Richard R. Dorr, Deputy Sheriff — Cook County, Minnesota

I've walked alone into the night
Sometimes to teach, sometimes to fight.

I can't begin to count the days
The path has turned so many ways.

A thought will cross my mind, can't speak
Am I perceived too tough, too weak?

There's been something there for everyone
Some choices haven't been much fun.

When troubles seem to never end
Try and recall, I've been your friend.

Please judge me fairly, if you can
Beneath this Badge.
      I'm just a man.

The Minnesota Police Journal

AUTHOR PROFILE

Richard 'Dick' Dorr is a retired
deputy sheriff. He worked four
years in Lyon County (Marshall),
Minnesota and twenty-two
years in Cook County (Grand
Marais) Minnesota serving
seventeen years as chief deputy. He graduated from Cook
County High School in 1966
and earned an AA degree from
Vermilion Community College

in Ely. He became a certified Minnesota peace officer in 1970.

Dick was active in the community. He was an original
member of the Cook County Booster Club and served as
president for twenty years. He volunteered for 25 years as a
color commentator for WTIP radio broadcasts of sporting
events.

Dick's career highlight was participating in an investi-
gation that led to solving a murder cold case in Michigan.
He received a commendation for his involvement from the
Michigan State Police.

Dick and his wife, Laurie, are now living in Hutchinson,
Minnesota.

BIBLIOGRAPHY SOURCES

Personal logbook and notes

Personal Interviews

Duluth Tribune

Cook County News Herald

Cook County Clerk of Courts Office

Cook County Recorder's Office

Grand Marais City Hall records

Grand Marais Public Library

Lake County Clerk of Courts Office

Minnesota Police & Police Officers Journal

ACKNOWLEDGEMENTS

My story began with a loving family. Florence, my mother, provided a safe Christian home. Ray, my father, was a lawman who shared insights and gave me advice that served me well in my career. He was my hero! At age 22, I met and married Laurie who has been everything to me. She gave me unconditional love, support, good advice and two sons-Mitch and Rich. They grew into young men who continue to enrich my life. Mitch married Sharon and they gave us four grandchildren-Adam, Jacob, Paul and Rachel.

I offer thanks to the sheriffs I worked for. To Emerson Morris who gave me an opportunity to begin my career. To John Tomasek in Lyon County for the educational opportunities to become a more complete officer. To John Lyght for offering me a chance to return to Cook County. To Dave Wirt for having the courage to effect change.

During my early career in Cook County, fellow deputies I worked with included Fred Schmidt, Ken Carlson, Myron Wilson, Steve Peterson, Kerry Beckenbach, Brian Sadler and Frank Redfield. The latter part of my career I worked with Tim Weitz, Dave Wirt, Leif Lunde, Doug Rude, Mark Falk and Pat Eliasen. These were officers who always answered calls professionally and promptly.

Our lifeline regarding communications in earlier years was Carol Weiss, Dolly Johnson, Florence Byholm and Carol

Wisneski. Nancy Backlund, Judy Sivertson, Edie Mattson, Geri Gecas, Lori Dimka, Barb Rierson and Joan Strandberg worked the latter part of my career. They were an outstanding group of dispatchers.

I will always remember longtime Grand Marais police officers Joe Jurek, Stan Suck and Jim Dalbec. I also remember Brian Cain and Kevin Kuschell. They served their community well.

County Attorney Richard Swanson offered good advice. We didn't always agree but there was mutual respect.

Judges Walt Eglund and Ken Sandvik were easy to work with when it came to search warrants. Telephonic search warrants were made possible thanks to Judge Eglund.

Very substantial career support came from Floyd Bowman and Joelle Kohout, agents with the Bureau of Criminal Apprehension in St. Paul. Thanks also to Duluth Police Chief Scott Lyons who assisted with the use of his investigators and crime lab facilities.

Thanks to Lois Johnson, head of Social Services and social worker Annie DeBevec along with Women's Advocate Sharon Karas. Thanks to probation officers Karen Onken and Steve Borud for their good work.

State Troopers-Jim Johnson, Jim Dols, Darren Fagerman, Lea Carpenter and especially Don Ziesmer who paid the ultimate sacrifice.

Game wardens-Bill Zickrick, Dan Ross, Al Heidebrink, Connie Tikala, Dan Cogswell who always offered assistance.

As the county services grew to meet demands, I thank the men and women of the volunteer fire departments, search and rescue squads throughout the county, and hospital health providers for their expertise and cooperation. There are not enough words to describe what they meant to the law enforcement community.

I received so much support in the back country, especially from lodge owners that included Frank Hansen from Sawbill Lodge, the Baumann family at Golden Eagle Lodge, the Kerfoots at Gunflint Lodge, the Austins at Rockwood Lodge, Don and Opal Enzenauer at Voyagers Landing on Seagull Rive,r and Pat Schunn on Saganaga Lake.

The men and women of the U.S. Forest Service provided incredible support with search and rescue missions and major support during the Rainbow invasion. State Foresters Ben Petz and Orvis Lunke probably walked every mile of Cook County forests and always assisted when called upon. The Sheriff's Department could count on support from U.S. Customs and U.S. Border Patrol officers as well as the U.S. Coast Guard.

A special thank you to Norman Deschampe, a great leader for the Grand Portage band of Lake Superior Ojibway. He was an outstanding visionary and good friend.

Finally, special appreciation to retired Sergeant Matthew T. Struck of the Hopkins Police Department for his thoughtful work on the Foreword of my book. Many thanks to my wife, Laurie, for her editing and additional input to my story. Special thanks to Richard Struck for his encouragement and editing skills. His expertise has been much appreciated.

Any omissions on my part are mine alone and unintentional.